BRETTLES OF BELPER

A history of a famous Derbyshire hosiery company and brand

Rod Hawgood and Gary Spendlove

Mayoral procession passing Mansion House, London.

BRETTLES OF BELPER

A history of a famous Derbyshire hosiery company and brand

Rod Hawgood and Gary Spendlove

ACKNOWLEDGEMENTS

First a confession: I never worked for Brettles. In fact, before I moved to Belper in 2006, it was just a name to me. Then I met Gary Spendlove, who had worked his way up through the ranks of George Brettle & Co. and now owned the brand – and he educated me. For the past year I have researched the history of the company, and am amazed how involved I have become. I now feel as though I was at least a 'fly on the wall' at every stage of its history, that each sports day or celebration event described is a good memory, and that every Works Manager's death was a personal loss.

I owe thanks to a number of people. First of all, on primary research, a big thank you to the staff of Belper North Mill Museum, especially to Natascha Wintersinger and Ray Marjoram, who have given me access to a large number of very relevant historical pictures and artefacts, and to renowned media photographer Nick Lockett for his services. Thanks to local historian Mary Smedley for her advice on the first chapter, helping to weed out some unconfirmed 'facts'. Thanks to the staff of Belper Library, of Derbyshire Records Office, and of the St John's Chapel Heritage Centre, having spent many hours at these worthy establishments, poring over books, documents and pictures.

I appreciate the earlier written accounts of various periods of Brettles' history, in particular, Negley Harte's exhaustive history of the original partnership and the first century of George Brettle & Co. For readers who would like a more detailed account than mine, especially of the financial progress and crises of the company, I would unhesitatingly direct them to Harte's book, '*A History of George Brettle & Co. 1801 - 1964*', compiled in 1973. I have also been glad of the story of 'Ward Brettle & Ward' written by William Ward and John Finney in 1823, for the much later summary history compiled in-house for the bicentennial 'Brettles Supplement' of the Belper News in 1986, and for the older articles in the *Derby Mercury*, *Derby Evening Telegraph*, *Derbyshire Advertiser*, *Hosiery Times* and *Womens Wear News*. For the most part these have corroborated and confirmed each other; where they have differed, it has been an interesting challenge to reconcile them.

I wish to thank those employees of Brettles, past and present, too many to mention here, who have taken the time to tell me their stories and memories of past years. As I have carefully woven these together, I hope the result forms a worthy tribute to these important chapters of Belper's history; and of their own. Finally, a very special tribute to my friend and colleague Gary Spendlove, who has made all this possible – both the presence of the Brettles brand in Belper today, and also this book, which was his brainchild. He has been my inspiration and enabler in the writing of it.

Rod Hawgood

CONTENTS

INTRODUCTION

Welcome to the history of George Brettle & Co. I decided to compile this book primarily because the Brettles brand of Belper has a place in history as one of the world's largest hosiery manufacturers. The company were also one of the UK's largest employers, employing well over one thousand people in the late 19th century. Of course, in our age of multi-nationals and international business, a company of this size would not be considered as significant as it was a hundred years ago. But it is worth stating that a company like Brettles would still create many thousands of hours of employment for associated and co-operating business, for example with packaging, labelling, marketing, photography, transport, etc. You could add to this the many processes of garment manufacture undertaken away from the site, such as spinning, weaving, knitting, dyeing, printing, assembly, etc. All of these processes still come together for distribution from our Belper head office.

The earliest records of the Brettle family and its association with textiles appear in the eighteenth century. There was an association with the Wards' factory in Belper until George Brettle founded his own highly successful business. It is not easy to estimate the wealth of George Brettle but his net income would have been between two and three million pounds a year as a modern-day equivalent figure. As with most businesses, the fortunes of the company fluctuated, but a 'golden period' in the 1930s helped the then chairman Harry Twyford become Alderman, Sheriff then Lord Mayor of London just before World War II. There is clear documentation that Sir Harry entertained many members of the British monarchy and royalty from other countries. A wide mixture of international VIPs were also hosted by the Brettles Chairman, even including members of the German Nazi Party!

After the 1940 destruction of the London headquarters in the Blitz, the focus of operations was the factory built by Brettle at Chapel Street, Belper, which continued until the move to Alfreton in 1987. A major change to the business occurred in 1964 when the company became part of the Courtaulds empire. Various management strategies ensured the continuation of the brand, predominantly through the distribution network of what was still called 'the London side'. A tripling of the company's turnover in the 1980s and 90s was again seen to be a strong period for the company under the management of Chief Executive Gwyn Stevenson.

Following a failed management buy-out bid in 1997, the business was sold to Leicester-based underwear manufacturer Chilprufe. This could have been the end of the Brettles story, but the later demise of Chilprufe allowed the Slenderella management to purchase the Brettle and associated brands from the administrator and realise a lifelong ambition to own the brand and return it to its historic home in Belper.

The Brettles name is a registered trademark and the brand enjoys continuing growth as part of the Slenderella group. It is sold to consumers via many retail outlets, mail order companies and internet businesses, and exported to a number of countries around the world.

At the start of my career, in a meeting between myself and Tony Gray, the then Managing Director, Tony impressed me with a phrase, saying 'We are custodians of the brand.' So I am pleased and proud to say that the Brettles brand is again secure in committed private ownership and in a strong position to expand onwards into the twenty-first century. I hope you enjoy the story.

Gary Spendlove

1. THE ORIGINS OF BRETTLES

The name 'Brettles' has been well known everywhere for socks, stockings, knitted goods and textiles, but nowhere more than in its home town of Belper in the Derwent Valley of Derbyshire, where the business has grown and matured for over 200 years. From tiny beginnings in the early nineteenth century, it survived more than its fair share of difficulties to become the biggest local employer, comparing very favourably with other companies in manufacturing capacity and output, numbers of looms and of hands employed. From Belper, its products went far and wide. In recent times under its present management the Brettles range has been updated and has gone on to achieve record exports. The history of Brettles is therefore an important part of the history of Belper.

Earliest Origins

The fascinating story goes back at least three hundred years. For by the early eighteenth century, the English hosiery industry was concentrated in the three East Midlands counties of Derbyshire, Nottinghamshire and Leicestershire. It had been in the Nottinghamshire village of Calverton that in 1589 the 'stocking frame' was invented by William Lee, a young clergyman not long returned from Cambridge to his own village. It was one of the most complicated pieces of technology known to the pre-industrial world, with over two thousand separate parts, but it became the crucial piece of machinery in the European hosiery industry for the next three centuries.

London, as the political, commercial and fashion centre of the country, was the main market for high-quality luxury knitted silk goods, and it was natural that most of the early frames were established there. It was in London that the Worshipful Company of Framework Knitters was formed in 1657 to control the new trade, but by the 1690s that company was fighting a losing battle to maintain its privileges against the rising hosiery industry of the East Midlands. By the 1720s, more of the country's 8,000 stocking frames were in the East Midlands than in the London area,[1] the main competitive advantages being the supply of cheap labour, along with lower rents, fuel and food prices, combined with proximity to the supply of wool. Then the first pair of cotton stockings made in England were produced in Nottingham, from imported Indian yarn.[2]

Within the East Midlands, Leicester came to specialise in wool, Nottingham in cotton, and Derby in silk. To supply silk to this growing industry, Thomas Lombe built his silk-throwing factory in Derby in 1718. And Derby was the birthplace of the most important development of Lee's stocking frame forty years later.

Seven miles north of Derby, Belper had until the mid eighteenth century been a village of little consequence, regarded as 'low in population as it was backward in civility . . . the insignificant residence of a few uncivilised nailers',[3] a poorly paid and typically family occupation. In 1741 there was estimated to be just 532 people living there, in 113 houses. But the development of textiles in Belper owes its origins to three families – the Strutts, the Arkwrights and the Wards.

Strutt and Arkwright

Jedediah Strutt, the son of a small farmer, was born in July 1726 at Blackwell, near Alfreton. His mother came from Hazelwood near Belper. Jedediah's mechanical and creative abilities surfaced early when he built a working windmill, and his father apprenticed him at 14 to a wheelwright called Ralph Massey at Findern, just south of Derby, where he lodged with the Woollat family. In this family he met his future wife Elizabeth and her brother William, who later became his business partner in the framework knitting trade. Strutt finished his apprenticeship in 1747, and was briefly a journeyman wheelwright in Leicester, before returning to Blackwell to take over a farm left to him by his uncle.

However, Strutt's mechanical interests were directed towards the framework knitting industry. In the long, low garret of his farmhouse, he produced an attachment to the machine invented by William Lee over 150 years earlier to knit a firm rib for hosiery (previously only done by hand). In about 1758 the family moved to Derby, where Strutt and William Woollat went into business in hosiery. That year, Strutt's 'Derby Rib Machine' was finished, and patented for seven years.

Strutt and Woollat imported raw silk via London and spun it in their new silk mill at Derby. The thread was distributed to small frame shops and outworkers' cottages by the 'Middlemen', and the finished products were sent back to London. They then diversified into yarn, which was cheaper and more durable. In the course of his trading, Strutt was in regular touch with the development in Nottingham of a steady market in cotton hosiery, using cotton yarn from Lancashire and went into partnership with Samuel Need of Nottingham.

In 1768 Strutt entered into partnership with Richard Arkwright,[4] who had just come from Lancashire to Nottingham, the growing centre for cotton hosiery, bringing his ideas for revolutionising the process of spinning the raw material. With the help of Strutt and Samuel Need, Arkwright patented the Water Frame. Following this, again with Strutt's backing, by 1771 he had built his famous water-powered cotton-spinning mill at Cromford, just south of Matlock, marking the beginning of the Industrial Revolution.

Above: View of Round Mill (built 1809) with Mule Room (1820), Reeling Mill (1807) at centre and Junction Mill (1810) right, from West Mill. (Photographer A N Smith 1959) Courtesy of Belper Historical Society.

Strutt now focused his attention on Belper, seven miles downstream from Cromford. Inspired by Arkwright, but frustrated by the quality of yarn available for his hosiery business, Strutt did the same there. Between 1776 and 1778, he built his first large cotton mill at Belper. He followed this with a second between 1784 and 1786 (North Mill) and a third between 1793 and 1795 (West Mill). And Strutt did more for Belper than build the mills: he provided a good deal of workers' housing, in streets opposite North Mill named 'Long Row', 'Short Row' and 'The Clusters'. He also built the Unitarian chapel in 1788. Strutt lived in Belper himself during the 1780s, then built a small mansion at Milford near his latest mill, just south of Belper.

Belper Bridge, North Mill & chimney (built 1852), about 1900. Courtesy of Belper Historical Society.

Bridge Foot, West Mill and the 1897 Jubilee Clock tower. Courtesy of Belper Historical Socity.

East Mill, Round Mill, The Gangway and offices, from West Mill. (Photographer A N Smith 1959). Courtesy of Belper Historical Society.

West Mill with Junction & other buildings since demolished (Photographer A N Smith 1962). Courtesy of Ray Marjoram and Belper Historical Society Collection.

From Belper to America

The textile revolution spread throughout the British Isles to Europe, and went much further, thanks to another son of Belper, one of Strutt's managers. Samuel Slater was born in 1768, in Blackbrook near Belper, the fifth son of William Slater. The family were Methodists, and Thomas Slater held services in their kitchen from 1767. They were involved when John Wesley visited Belper in 1782 and 1786 and preached in the Market Place. The Central Methodist Church was built in 1807, and 'John Slater' built a chapel at Blackbrook in 1816.

Samuel Slater started a six-year apprenticeship with Strutt in 1782, at age 14, working in his Belper Mill, during which he found a way to wind more cotton onto a bobbin. Strutt was pleased with him and trained him to oversee the making of cotton frames, and later to help manage the construction of his new factory at Milford. Slater also helped Strutt in arranging the purchase of land and of water rights for this project.

However, Slater came across a newspaper from Philadelphia, USA in which he read of the generous bounties offered in the States to encourage manufacture. In 1789 he went to London and bought his passage to New York, a voyage that took 66 days. He found the American textile industry very much in its infancy, with water power unknown and cotton spinning still done by treadmill and donkey wheel, giving an uneven and lumpy yarn. His landlord was a blacksmith, and it was advantageous that Slater had experience of manufacturing machine parts. In great demand due to his experience, in January 1790 he started as a Manager for Moses Brown, a Quaker, with his company Almy & Brown at

Pawtucket, where he built a mill on the Arkwright model, which was claimed to be the first factory in America. This involved using some trade secrets learned from Strutt, and consequently he became known in Belper as 'Slater the Traitor' and took delight in sending a sample of his products to Strutt! In 1791 he married Hannah Wilkinson, daughter of his landlord, and in 1798 he entered a new partnership with his in-laws as Samuel Slater & Co., and also started a Sunday School for the children of the workers. How interesting that over two hundred years later, the towns of Belper and Pawtucket USA are twinned – any rivalry that may have once existed long since replaced by this expression of the 'special relationship' between the two countries

Samuel Slater and his factory in America (Photographer: Nick Lockett).

From Village to Town

Back in the Derwent Valley, the building of mills continued apace. During the last quarter of the eighteenth century a string of textile mills were built along the Derwent between Matlock and Derby. These inevitably changed the predominant employment from agricultural to industrial and increased the valley's population. Strutt lived at Milford in his closing years; he died in 1797 and was buried in the chapel at Delper which he had built just nine years earlier.

Strutt's sons, William, George and Joseph Strutt, continued the family business as 'W.G. & J. Strutt', and their cotton-spinning mills were the centre of the community. William had been with his father in the business for many years and now pioneered the much-needed fireproof mills as a response to the frequent fires. His first was built at Derby in 1793. In 1803 Belper's wood-framed North Mill burnt down, but William rebuilt it the following year to his revolutionary design, being iron-framed throughout, one of the first such buildings.[5] William's designs were also used in Derby buildings, such as the Infirmary built in 1810, which employed a heating system used in North Mill. He designed the St Mary's Bridge and other bridges, including one at Milford for access to the mills.

The coming of the mills had transformed Belper into a factory town. The first census, in 1801, recorded a population that had grown more than eightfold from 532 to 4,500 in just 60 years. By then it was considered to be 'one of the most flourishing places in Derbyshire', its population exceeding any town in the county except Derby itself. It then reached 5,778 by 1811, 7,235 by 1821, and slowed to 7,890 in 1831. A second spurt brought it to 9,885 in 1841, then it slowed to 10,082 by 1851, at which point it plateaued and stabilised for the next century.

Meanwhile the Strutts continued to invest in Belper philanthropically, building the town's first school (and one in Derby), which employed teachers and 'pupil teachers'. They later contributed in a large way to the cost of the new Anglican church of St Peter built between 1822 and 1824, replacing the small St John's Chapel, which is now a heritage centre. Church growth accompanied population growth in Belper, with the Central Methodist Church already established, Christ Church built in 1850 near the mills, the Congregational Church in 1872 and the Baptist Church in 1894, as well as smaller churches on the outskirts such as Pottery Methodist Church.

The Wards

Focussing in on hosiery, the Brettles story begins with John Ward senior, who in the second half of the eighteenth century carried on a hosiery business in Belper. It is unclear when this began, but in a letter to a prospective customer in 1812 his son stated, 'Our house is upon an establishment of 50 years' standing. We therefore do not spring up as new adventurers, in soliciting your orders' – which suggests it went back at least to 1762. In another letter two years later, he referred to men at Windley who up to 25 years earlier had been 'working to' his father, therefore in the 1780s.[6]

John Ward's mother had been a Strutt of Newton, near Blackwell in Derbyshire, and his sister Elizabeth married John Strutt, possibly the brother of the famous Jedediah Strutt.[7] So the two families were related before the latter became a successful Derby hosier, and before his partnership with Arkwright and the building of the spinning mill in 1776 that was to

Above: 'Kilburn Cheveners on Danesbury Rise, 'Denby Bottles', 1920' and **left:** 'Group of Cheveners, Mrs E.A. Gamble of Ripley (born 1905) on right, 1913'.

so utterly transform the community of Belper. Such family connections were important in business life, and significantly, a 'Mr. Ward' helped Arkwright with the building of the original Cromford Mill.[8]

It was very relevant to the Wards business that there were already many independent home-based handloom workers around Belper, and it was also a centre of 'chevening' (called 'clocking' by the London guilds), which was the embroidery onto stocking sides of a simple standard design resembling a lamp post with two branching legs. 'Clocked' stockings are over four hundred years old, for Queen Elizabeth I is reputed to have worn similar pairs of embroidered hose. This was a cottage industry, which was developed to produce a range of beautiful intricate designs embroidered onto stockings and socks. The source of the word 'chevening' is uncertain; one explanation is that it came from France, brought over by the French silk workers. Another attractive explanation is that it comes from the Chevin Ridge on the edge of Belper. Certainly, an old word that used to be used in Belper was 'chevir', meaning 'bring to a head'. The operation of 'clocking' or chevening involved bringing a thread of embroidery up the leg of a stocking to its head, using a blunted needle. The cheveners joined the seam of the stocking by hand in its undyed, unfinished state.[9]

The marriage register shows that on 16th April 1759, John Ward had married Susannah Bradley, the daughter of Benjamin Bradley, a well-to-do yeoman farmer of Belper.[10] This marriage produced seven children, the oldest being John junior, who was involved in the business by the early 1790s, since he was to write in 1812 that he had been making fashioned drawers 'for more than twenty years',[11] and by 1799 the firm was known as 'Ward & Son', a partnership business.[12] The Wards were big customers of the Strutts. Ledgers show that in 1799, the Wards were buying yarn worth some £20 per month from the cotton-spinning North Mill, and in the following year these yarn purchases increased substantially to average £60 per month.[13]

By 1801, John senior had retired, and his place was taken in the partnership business by James Carter Sharp of Duffield (just south of Belper). As 'Ward Sharp and Co.' they opened a warehouse in the City of London at 6 Cateaton Street.[14] There, a William Bacon was employed to sell their hosiery products to the retailers. Previously they would have sold to one of the larger hosiers, the wholesale or merchant hosiers who acted as middlemen between the producer and the retailer. Now, Ward and Sharp were able to deal with retailers direct, and could claim, as they did to a London retail customer in January 1802, that they 'charged you the same prices as we sell to the wholesale warehouses in town (who serve the retail shopkeepers). We therefore judge it is a thing impossible for them to sell you the same qualities at the same prices.'[15]

Following this important move into wholesale and into the London market, the firm seems to have initially undergone a considerable expansion. In 1802 their purchases of yarn from the Strutts totalled £1,475, an average of over £120 per month, twice as much as in 1800.

However, it would seem that this spurt was not maintained, and that problems arose at the London end. Customer complaints were received in 1802; John Ward claimed that 'complaints are both novel and unpleasant to us'. But when James Sharp went to London in 1803 to survey the affairs at that end, he was deeply dissatisfied. Indeed, in the words of John Ward's brother William, he was 'incensed at the manner in which they had been conducted' and the effects on the business, so much so that he 'determined upon withdrawing himself from the partnership'.[16]

John's brother William Ward was at this time employed in another London hosiery warehouse at 1 Milk Street, near Cateaton Street, which was owned by Thomas Smith and Sons. He knew of the problems and also that his brother John was 'individually insolvent' and that he was 'under arrest at the suit of Mr. Arkwright for about £700 or £800, in whose favour judgement was suffered to go by default for a debt contracted . . . previously to his partnership with Mr. Sharp'.[17] William therefore became alarmed for the consequences for John and for the family if the business had to be wound up abruptly, and he began to seriously consider 'whether any possible means could be found of saving his brother from approaching destruction'.[18] In seeking to offer a rescue deal, his thoughts turned to George Brettle, who like himself, was living in the house of Thomas Smith and Sons in London, and whom he regarded as of 'integrity and perseverance'.

Enter George Brettle

Nothing is known of the earlier years of George Brettle. Stories prevalent later in the firm were that he had been a Belper framework knitter, or that he began making stockings at Ilkeston in 1782, and that he rode to London in 1787 to sell his stockings, but these dates are discounted by the one known fact that he was born on 1st January 1778 (so he would have been a child prodigy!). There is therefore no firm evidence of any previous time spent living or working in Belper.

An article in the *Derby Evening Telegraph* of 5th March 1954 records that George Brettle's father Edward had been in business in Cateaton Street (now Gresham Street) as 'E. Brettle and Co. – haberdashers and merchants', and established the brand 'House of Brettle' in 1786, probably never dreaming that its bicentennial anniversary would be celebrated at Belper in 1986.

George Brettle served his seven-year apprenticeship with Thomas Smith and Sons in Milk Street, living with the other apprentices in the domestic quarters attached to the Smiths' warehouse. By this means he became a neighbour and colleague of William Ward – and the rest, as they say, is history.

2. GEORGE BRETTLE AND THE WARDS

In 1803 a crucial meeting took place – William Ward introduced George Brettle to his brother John as 'the means of rescuing John from his fearful situation'. As a result, on 21ˢᵗ July 1803 the new partnership of 'Ward Brettle & Ward' was formed by Brettle and the Wards to take over the business, assets and liabilities of Ward Sharp & Co. It was found that net assets totalled £3,067, of which £567 was to be credited to John Ward and £2,500 to James Sharp, who, however, allowed his capital to remain in the new partnership, in exchange for annual interest of 5 per cent and an allowance of £150 for seven years, after which time the sum was to be repaid in full. There was not even any cash in hand, just some stocking frames, a quantity of unsold stock and some book debts. Neither George Brettle nor William Ward brought any capital to the partnership, only a knowledge of the trade and the capacity to work hard, though they had the use of the Wards' Belper warehouse in Derby Road and the leased warehouse at Cateaton Street, London from the old Ward Sharp & Co.

On top of this uninspiring collection of assets, the bills accepted by Ward Sharp & Co. were daily becoming due, and there was also the problem of William Bacon, the warehouse manager, who had earlier been promised continued employment under such terms as could have constituted partnership in the eyes of the law. Indeed, shortly afterwards a bill was drawn by John Ward upon 'Ward, Brettle & Ward & Co.' and in explanation John Ward stated that the '& Co.' was intended for Bacon, John having promised that he would appear to the world as a partner![1]

In the view of William and George, Bacon was 'a man of broken fortunes and totally without credit', in more ways than one. They sacked him, and consequently one of the first things the new firm had to face was a bill in Chancery filed against them by Bacon. The beginnings of Ward, Brettle and Ward were far from auspicious.

The new partnership was surrounded by what William Ward called 'difficulties of the most appalling and distressing description', including the legacy debts, new bills arriving every week and the nightmare of litigation. Reflecting on the period, George Brettle wrote: 'I know and have experienced the racks and torments of embarrassed finances', and later he described it as 'the most anxious and painful course that men ever passed through'.[2]

Amazing Growth

Despite this, the dominant theme of the 30 years after 1803 was expansion, whether measured by the number of frames, of people employed, the range of goods produced or dealt in, by turnover, profit or assets – all told the same story.[3] In the first decade of the nineteenth century, each new frame cost from £25 to £50 depending on size, and a second-hand one £10. But partnership assets were £3,067 in 1803, £4,160 in 1805 and grew to £8,544 by late 1807.

The business became a valued employer in Belper. In late 1808, John Ward informed a customer that they had 'seven to eight hundred workmen constantly at work'. More were taken on in each of the following years, including 1812 when trade was briefly depressed. In November 1812 John Ward could claim that 'we have in our employ for several years upwards of one thousand workmen, consequently we make a great variety of sorts, we believe more than any other house in the trade'.

Pre-Factory Production

It should be explained that right up to about 1850, hosiery production was mainly a domestic industry. Most of the knitting machines owned by Brettles, as by the other hosiers, remained hand frames worked in the operatives' dwelling houses or in small workshops attached to them. In 1823, there were only 33 frames at the Belper warehouse. The remainder were in workshops up to 25 miles away from Belper. Ward Brettle & Ward frames could be found as far north as Wessington, Alfreton and Sutton-in-Ashfield, and as far east as Heanor and the suburbs of Nottingham, the places from whence stockingers later gave evidence to an 1844 inquiry. These domestic workshops contained between two and six frames, and sometimes up to ten.[4] Another special group of outworkers employed around Belper were the 'cheveners', who embroidered designs onto stockings and socks.

Journeymen, travelling on horseback, were employed to deliver the yarn from the Belper warehouse to these workshops each week, then to bring the almost-completed stockings back for linking and seaming. Then the finished goods were taken by coach and horses, or by pack-horses, mainly to the London warehouse, apart from some to customers in the Midlands and North.[5]

Marjorie Blount records that for the first two decades of the nineteenth century, many stockings were brought into Belper in bulk by carrier's cart from Nottingham to the warehouse, then collected and distributed by 'chevening mistresses' to the local women on their books. Often women would not receive their work until three in the afternoon, and it would be required for despatch early the next morning. One could often see rows of women, 'sitting in their doorways of their homes in order to catch the last of the light, with starched white aprons crackling and their bobbin-stands humming as they spun and threaded the silk', then often sitting at their table late into the night, with a lamp pulled close, intent and absorbed in her work. Every Saturday morning the mistresses could be seen 'carrying neat white bags, notebook in hand, going to collect their money'.[6]

Factory production, such as characterised the late eighteenth century, was unknown in the hosiery business at that time. The term 'manufactory' was sometimes used, and this incorporated both the warehouse and the multiplicity of small domestic workshops which were either outbuildings to or on the top floor of the framework knitters cottages.

The rapid advance in the number of framework knitters employed was matched by extensions to the firm's warehouse space. In 1812 the Belper premises were referred to as having been 'lately enlarged', and in 1809 or 1810 new larger London warehouse premises were taken at 119 Wood Street, replacing Cateaton Street, which was to remain the London address for the next 130 years. Wood Street formed part of that area north-east of St Paul's Cathedral which was the 'heart of London' for textile interests. There were many other hosiery houses, textile warehouses and a variety of dealers in goods such as lace, silk and ribbons. It was in nearby Gutter Lane in 1828 that Samuel Courtauld & Co. took their first London premises, the forerunners of the Courtaulds empire that would one day acquire the Brettles business – but that was still well over a century ahead.

In London, unlike Belper, a large number were employed within the warehouse, and discipline was strict. There was in fact even a 'scold's bridle' for use as a punitive measure for over-talkative women'! There was an article about it entitled 'Old Time Bridle' in the *Yarns* magazine of 1929, though it was already viewed as a curiosity that was last used 'many years ago'.[7]

Products

It would also be useful at this point to review the extent of the partnership's product range. The term 'hosiery' defined products made from yarn, whether silk, cotton or woollen, by the process of knitting. Usually wool or worsted was used in the Leicester area, cotton in the Nottingham area, and silk in the Derby area. The main hosiery products were stockings (called 'hose' in the trade) and socks (called 'half-hose', 'socks' being the term reserved for children's socks). The leading products of the Belper establishment were cotton stockings of various sorts – plain and ribbed, white, black and coloured, coarse and fine. They also made or dealt in pantaloons, drawers, gloves and caps.

In the first quarter of the nineteenth century, the number of drapers greatly increased. Drapers dealt primarily in pieces of cloth – whether woollen, cotton or linen – for the home production of clothing and bedding. They also kept a certain amount of ready-made clothing, hats, gloves and various hosiery, besides a multiplicity of threads, tapes, ribbons and trimmings that went by the name of haberdashery. It was to cater directly for this growing breed of trader that the wholesaling side of the partnership had been established. In addition to their own products, to supply their 'extensive connection among the retail linen drapers', the partnership also dealt in haberdashery and in various woollen piece-goods, sourced from the Manchester area and made from Yorkshire wool.

Over the first twenty years, many Ward Brettle & Ward customers outside London and the Home Counties were served direct from Belper, especially those in the Midlands and Yorkshire. The regular coach service between Birmingham and Sheffield passed through Belper, and was used to transport smaller quantities to both places. Goods were also sent by the wagons of Pickfords and other carriers to Liverpool, including some for shipment to Dublin. But from the mid 1820s it became normal to take all products to the London warehouse and then dispatch them from there. For example, a new Birmingham customer in 1822 had his order sent via London, 'from which place', it was explained, 'we shall prefer executing your orders, as we can do it more expeditiously and equally as advantageous to you in price as if sent from our manufactory, being in the habit of forwarding three or four times every week our goods as they come to hand to our London warehouse'.[8]

Wards factory, relatively recent, possibly by Fred Robson, courtesy of Belper Historical Society.

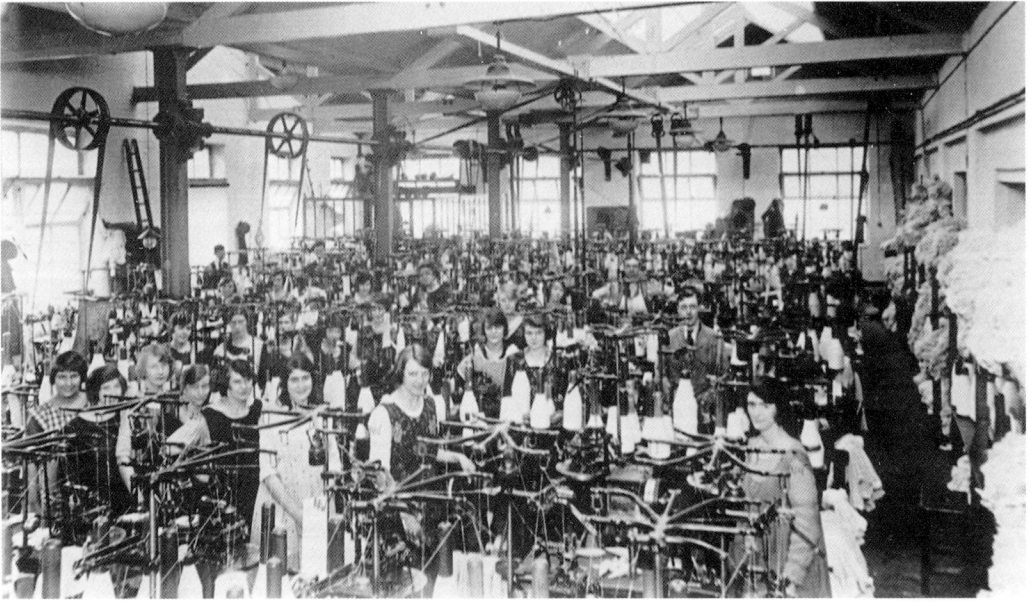

Wards workroom, Derby Road, about 1914, photographer unknown.

Above and opposite page: Wards workrooms, postcards by H Burkinshaw before 1919
Courtesy of Ray Marjoram and Belper Historical Society Collection.

'Trouble at Mill'

All, however, was not well between the partners – George Brettle and William Ward, the London partners, fell out with John Ward, the Belper partner. A dispute arose in 1823 over the way in which John was dealing with the Derbyshire stocking makers and over some building alterations. The Belper warehouse was mainly owned by John Ward, rent being paid by the partnership after 1803 for its use. John was building a new 'Trim Shop' there, a place in which the finishing processes were to be undertaken on the knitted goods, and was charging this work to the partnership. In Brettle's view this cost should have been met by John Ward as owner, or, if not, then arrangements should have been made for the others to share in the value of such buildings in the event of dissolution of the partnership. George wrote to him on 17th July 1823 that these alterations were 'simply to please your fancy' and that the business should not be charged, and also alleging irregularities in John's conduct of his end of the business, in that he had taken some £150 'out of the trade cash for his own use and not posted it to his debit'. John did not reply to this letter, and George wrote again on 28th July. This elicited an offer to 'stop the new erections' and a plea of unfair treatment. Then, on 9th August, John Ward offered to withdraw from the partnership.

A period of recrimination was then unleashed. In early September, John Ward wrote to George Brettle, superciliously in the third person:

> JW after twenty years acquaintance hopes he may presume to say that it would give him great pleasure to see GB in the same spirit he was in ten years ago. The increase of riches has certainly brought with it an undue increase of avarice, not only perceptible to JW but he has heard it noticed by customers.

Four days later, George Brettle responded in the same vein:

> In regard to GB's avarice, he thinks he may fairly shake hands with his worthy friend JW on that score. He has however the satisfaction to think that he has never indulged that passion at the expense of another mans labour.[9]

William Ward hurried to Belper to attempt a reconciliation, but John would have none of it. William, entirely in agreement with George Brettle, reluctantly recorded that they had both always felt that 'no reliance whatever could be placed on the co-operation of John Ward'. The firm's difficulties in its early years were in his view 'greatly aggravated by the total indifference which John Ward at all times displayed, even on the most trying occasions. Not only so but he even increased these distresses by making purchases of land and houses at the time when the necessities of the firm were the most severely pressing'.

The dispute was exacerbated by John Ward's insistence that Benjamin Bradley Ward, the youngest of the three Ward brothers, should replace him as partner. Benjamin had some years previously been unsuccessful in his own business, having managed in two years to lose not only £700 of his own money but the £1,000 business capital that 'Ward, Brettle & Ward' had lent him. He had then been employed by the partnership 'by way of asylum for him' and upon the express assurance to George Brettle that it should be 'at a modest salary'.

But William Ward stated that 'Benjamin Ward is by no means a person who would be the object of our free choice. We do not consider him by any means competent to the management of our concern, and he would consequently be a dead weight on us by perpetuation of a tax on our industry.'[10] Thus both Brettle and William Ward now categorically refused to have him as a partner, objecting to such 'dictation' by John Ward and feeling that they could run the firm by themselves. But as a sop they agreed to raise his salary to £400.

John Ward left the partnership on 18th September 1823, gave up his claim that Benjamin should succeed him, and allowed the remaining two partners the continued use of the Belper warehouse. He left his £31,506 share of the business almost entirely in the hands of the other two partners, with agreed terms that it be repaid at the end of ten years, and that in the meantime he would be paid 5 per cent annual interest, a concession that George Brettle felt was 'a terrible tax upon our future industry'. John retired to Cheltenham 'to attend to the restoration of his injured health'.

It may seem surprising that a family that had supported each other so loyally at their own cost – rescuing first John then Benjamin Ward – should fall out so badly, and more so that one of them, William, should side with a family outsider in preference to his own brothers. But no doubt he had good reasons. 'Contracts of partnership,' wrote Brettle, 'like those of marriage, must spontaneously flow from the feelings and the will.' Referring to William, he wrote: 'That our partnership should have endured so long and with so much harmony is a thing almost without parallel in the commercial world.' It might have been expected at this stage that the business name would have been simplified to 'Brettle and Ward', but this did not happen; it continued as 'Ward Brettle & Ward', perhaps at William Ward's request to leave the road open for another sibling to join in the future.

Left: Rear of Brook Cottage adjacent to Wards factory, where John then Benjamin Ward lived, showing the mill chimneys.

Below: Early picture of Brook Cottage, with the Smith family, 1800-1810. (Courtesy of Ray Marjoram and Belper Historical Society).

Growth and Prestige

Despite the payments to John Ward, business growth accelerated under the management of the two remaining partners. They turned a £14.6k net loss in 1822 into a £7k (9.2%) net profit the following year, which grew to 17.3 per cent and to a peak of nearly £22k net profit in 1827.

Products by now went all over the British Isles, and to mainland Europe and even America. And in addition to the main range of hosiery, the firm also produced silk stockings, which in those days were exclusive to the nobility and to royalty. They made silk stockings for King George III, silk stockings and socks for George IV, the stockings worn by Queen Victoria on her Coronation day, and cotton stockings made for Queen Marie of Spain. Similarly with quality underwear, they made the vest that Lord Nelson was wearing when he met his death at Trafalgar, which is still preserved at Greenwich.

In 1824 the firm owned 269 stocking frames in Belper.[11] But in 1829 Stephen Glover, a local commercial investigator, noted that the growth of the business had made the business 'the most extensive hosiers in the kingdom'. In addition to large quantities of ordinary hosiery, they produced '2000 dozen pairs of silk hose weekly and little less than one hundred thousand dozens yearly'. He later wrote: 'Messrs Ward Brettle & Ward of Belper are esteemed to be the most extensive manufacturers of hosiery goods in the world. They employ about 400 silk stocking frames . . . besides 2,500 cotton hose frames.'[12]

Luxury at Brixton

From owning next to nothing at the beginning of the nineteenth century, the partners made themselves wealthy men. In 1803 they had been collectively net debtors to the extent of nearly £2,000. By 1823, when John Ward left the firm, his share was worth over £31,000, and ten years later the shares of George Brettle and William Ward were worth £117,839 and £115,992 respectively. The annual salaries they had originally allowed themselves from the business were £91 and £105 respectively. By 1820, George's salary had already grown to £900, at a time when the threshold of the middle classes was put at £250 per year, from which it was possible to employ at least one servant. By the end of the decade George was receiving £1,400 per annum, and William similarly, enabling them to become 'gentlemen' in the upper reaches of the expanding middle class – and such was the life that they grew to lead, if one can judge by the houses they bought for themselves.

In about 1817 George Brettle established himself at Raleigh Lodge, a substantial residence with fifteen acres of land on Brixton Hill in Surrey, on what was then the southern edge of London. Here he could enjoy what at the time was called the 'remarkably pure' air of Brixton, where many 'elegant seats and villas' were just beginning to be built, while being less than five miles from the firm's warehouse in Wood Street.[13] At about the same time he married a wife, Mary, who bore him two daughters, then three sons between 1819 and 1822.

Likewise, in the early 1820s William Ward became a resident of Cornwall Terrace, one of the grandiose Corinthian edifices newly erected by James and Decimus Burton to complete Nash's splendid plans for Regent's Park. Less than three miles from the Wood Street warehouse, William could enjoy the illusion of living in a magnificent mansion in a landscaped rural park. *The Gentleman's Magazine* referred to him as 'William Ward Esq. of Cornwall Terrace, Regent's Park and Wood Street, Cheapside, a very eminent wholesale hosier.'[14]

Left: Picture of Mrs. Mary Brettle (Courtesy of Ray Marjoram and Belper Historical Society Collection).

Death of the Partners

But monetary wealth and material luxury are only for this life; death comes to hovels and palaces alike. In his palatial house at Regent's Park, on 29th August 1833, William Ward died at the age of 58. His death activated an agreement he had reached with Brettle in 1827, which provided that neither the business nor the surviving partner should suffer in the event of the death of either of them. Ward's share was valued at the time of his death as £123,083/4/1d, and Brettle agreed to pay this to Anne Ward, William's widow, over ten years, with annual interest of 5 per cent. Even for someone in Brettle's position, payments on such a scale could not be easily made.

And so it was that George Brettle became the sole remaining partner. William had no children. Benjamin Ward, who had remained as the Belper factory manager, then made a fresh bid to become a partner in place of William, which was again refused. Realising that a serious rift was now likely, in February 1834 George purchased a piece of land known as 'The Croft' almost opposite the Belper warehouse, which had been owned by John Slater, a Shottle farmer. Then, to give a clear message, he changed the name of the concern to 'George Brettle & Co.' and wrote to all suppliers and customers accordingly on 7th August 1834. Later that month, Benjamin Ward issued a disingenuous contradictory circular, saying that his brother had died intestate, and that the manufacture of hosiery would be carried out at the same address as it had for many years, 'the last ten of which has been under my own immediate superintendence'. George Brettle responded with a corrective saying that for the last ten years he and William Ward were the only partners and that business would in future be conducted under the name of George Brettle & Co.[15]

From this point, production at the old premises became a breakaway rival concern. John Ward resurrected his business acquaintance with James Carter Sharp, his original partner of 1802, with his brother Benjamin and one 'Sturt', and the separate firm that they started became 'Ward Sturt & Sharp', producing in the original 'Ward Brettle & Ward' factory in Belper and using Leak Smith & Jones as their main selling agents, then renting their own London premises in Wood Street.

The loss of the Belper warehouse must have been a big blow to George Brettle. Many goods supplied by the business were not their own produce, so sourcing these would not have been affected, but with their own manufacturing resources at Belper and only the London warehouse remaining, maintaining quality and continuity of stock must have been a nightmare. George could have taken this opportunity to manufacture elsewhere in the country, but chose to continue doing so in Belper for commercial and economic reasons. A known and experienced workforce was crucial.

It should be remembered that at this time hosiery production was still mainly a domestic industry. At the time of the parting of the ways, most of the knitting machines remained hand frames worked in the operatives homes in the area around Belper.[16] So the loss of a warehouse did not mean the loss of the productive assets.

Many of the pre-1834 frames had belonged to the partnership and therefore now belonged to George Brettle. For these, all that had to be altered was the arrangement for the delivery of yarn and the collection and destination of finished goods, so the damage to George Brettle's manufacturing capacity would have been limited. But most of the frames belonged to individual stockingers or bagmen; these workers with their own frames would have had a choice as to who they worked for.[17] Many may have thought it less risky to produce for the existing Belper mill (the Wards), and daily life for these stockingers would have continued unchanged. We do not know how many transferred allegiance – no doubt incentives would have been offered by both sides, but unfortunately there appears to be no record of this.

Clearly, Brettle's new building at 'The Croft' had to be erected very quickly. The first stone was laid in May 1834 and it was completed by June 1835. New staff would have been recruited, or old staff re-employed. And so, after a ten months' gap, Brettles had a Belper base once again, and anyone travelling from Derby through Belper would have passed between the two rival concerns, together no doubt employing a large percentage of Belper residents. It is interesting that both in Belper and in London, as is often the case with rival banks today, the two had adjacent premises.

Then disaster struck – after just four months' production at the new factory, George Brettle suddenly died on 18th October 1835. Like William Ward at his time of death, he was only 58, and now the business was totally denuded of top management, with no partners left, and also a new cashflow problem. Only two payments had been made to Anne Ward, and under the terms of the agreement, the whole balance now became due in six months. How could the business survive such a plight?

But survive it did, for George Brettle had provided for just such a situation, and his family were also committed to the continuation of the business. In the will made four months before his death, George had stipulated that a £20,000 share be left to his wife and £10,000 to each of his daughters, and the remainder of his estate and management of his business be left in the hands of three friends, 'upon trust to carry out my trade and business of a wholesale hosier and manufacturer of hosiery now carried on in Wood Street, Cheapside and at Belper …'.[18] The three trustees were to be John Samson of Broad Street, Cheapside, Thomas Stokes, a wholesale hosier of Leicester, and Benjamin Hardwick, a solicitor of Cateaton Street. They were intended to operate the business until Brettle's youngest son attained the age of 21, enabling all sons to become partners.

But early in 1836, soon after the will had been proved, John Samson and Thomas Stokes both renounced the powers and rights that Brettle had conferred on them, leaving Benjamin Hardwick as the sole trustee. He somehow managed the business, while continuing to practise as a solicitor in the partnership of Hardwick and Davidson close to the Wood Street premises. The three Brettle sons were employed in the business, but under the terms of their father's will they were not allowed to undertake any decision-making or management in those years.

So it was not a good situation. Both partners dead, no full-time top management, a partly 'new' workforce at Belper whose loyalty and reliability had yet to be tested, and an immediate big debt to William Ward's widow. That the business survived the 1830s is nothing short of a miracle.

One person who seems to have given some continuity was Thomas Wilson Elstob, who had worked for the firm since 1827. For some years he had been manager of the 'counting house department' and had been George Brettle's 'confidential clerk'.[19] It would appear that he then played a crucial role in the management of the Belper manufactory during the period of Benjamin Hardwick's trusteeship. Trusted by the Brettle family, who expressed their 'utmost confidence in his integrity', he was destined to become a partner alongside the Brettles' sons.

3. UNDER THE BRETTLE BROTHERS

The year before his death, George Brettle had renamed his firm 'George Brettle & Co.', signifying a final break with the Ward family. His son George Henry must have been very happy about this name, and would eventually become the sole owner. But that was some years ahead – all was now in place for the three sons to become equal partners. After eight years of management by trusteeship, in 1843 George Brettle's three sons succeeded to their partnerships. Edward was 24, George Henry was 23 and Alfred was 21, and they

Above: Brettles Fire Engine, manufactured 1840.

made Thomas Elstob into the fourth partner without obliging him to provide any capital.[1]

The firm that the Brettle brothers inherited in 1843 was a prosperous one, though in output it had not yet made up the ground lost to the Wards business nine years earlier. Back in 1829 they were said to have employed 400 silk frames and 2,500 cotton frames, so 2,900 in total.[2] In 1844, Brettles had 'about 300 to 500' silk frames and only 'about 2,000' cotton frames, so at least 500 cotton frames fewer than before.[3] Meanwhile, the Wards firm had grown to a peak of about 4,000 frames, though only about half of these were owned, the rest belonging to individual stocking-makers or 'bagmen'. That firm was described by the Parliamentary Commissioner in 1844 as 'the most extensive manufacturers of hosiery in the kingdom'.[4]

By this time, it does seem that the two Belper companies were about the largest of their kind in the country. For comparison, in 1844 the well-known hosier Samuel Fox of Derby employed 700 frames.[5] One Nottingham hosier claimed to be 'perhaps as large a frame-holder as any individual in the country' when he employed 700 frames.[6] In 1841, William Felkin referred to the largest house in the trade as employing 3,000 frames, the second 2,000, a third and fourth about 1,800 each and a fifth employing 1,500.[7] Almost certainly the two biggest were the Wards and Brettles of Belper, followed by the two leading Nottingham firms, Hurst Sons & Ashwell, who employed 2,000 frames in 1844, and I. & R. Morley, who employed 2,700 frames in 1854.[8]

The domestic system of production suited both 'man and master', and the number employed was very much greater than the number of frames. 'The principal part of the framework knitters' family', stated one Belper stockinger in 1844, 'are employed in their business.'[9] Thomas Whittaker McCallum, the manager of Wards' cotton department, indicated that the 4,000 frames they employed created employment not only for 4,000 framework knitters, but also for about 2,000 seamers, 800 winders, 100 frame-smiths, needle-makers and sinker-makers, 100 dyers and bleachers, 300 embroiderers or cheveners, and 200 minders, trimmers and makers up – a total of some 3,500 in addition to the knitters themselves.[10]

Furthermore, size and quality apparently went hand in hand. Benjamin Morley of Nottingham stated in 1844 that the two Belper companies and his own 'make the best goods'. Referring to a market trend towards cheaper products, he complained that the threat to top-quality lines 'bears more upon ourselves and the two Belper houses than all the rest put together'.[11]

The Life of the Brothers

Like their father before them, the three brothers established themselves as 'gentlemen', whose lives were not restricted by the need to be over-involved in the day-to-day business of dealing in hosiery.

Of the three brothers, Alfred seems to have been considered the 'black sheep' of the family, and lived a stylish but unstable life. He was apparently married five days after his 21st birthday in 1843, but his wife died after two years. By 1852 he was living at Combe Hay House, a fine mansion in a wooded valley in Somerset, a few miles south of Bath. In 1855 he moved to an address off Park Lane in London, and the following summer to a residence in the Champs Elysées in Paris. There, in somewhat mysterious circumstances, he died in October 1856, aged only 34. It was officially stated that he died of epilepsy, but it appears that in reality his death was the result of falling out of his carriage after drinking too much champagne at the Chantilly races. He left most of his money to a 'Mrs Sophie Cunningham' and her children. A report of Chancery proceedings of 1864 refers to her as Alfred Brettle's daughter, but it seems very unlikely for a man of 34 to have a married daughter, let alone one with three children.[12] An air of mystery surrounds his life and death. Be that as it may, Edward and George Henry Brettle had to repay his share, which was valued at £57,447, and did so at the rate of £3,829 per annum from 1857, plus 4 per cent interest on the outstanding sum.

Edward Brettle, the eldest brother, remained a bachelor. He lived for a time in Regent Street, before taking the lease of an elegant flat in the Albany, off Piccadilly, in 1850. His account book shows that he took a large salary from the business and his expenditure levels were very high from the start – £1,909 in 1844, £1,765 in 1845, £3,593 in 1846, then never less than £3,000 in the ensuing years up to 1860. He paid regular subscriptions to the City of London Club, the Royal Yacht Club, the Society of Arts, the Surrey Reform Registration Society, and contributed £200 to the Patriotic Fund at the beginning of the Crimean War. By his forties, he had a grand country residence and a substantial estate at Henley Park in Surrey, between Aldershot and Guildford.[13] But he died on 20th May 1867 aged 47, as the *Derby Mercury* said, 'after a lingering illness of cancer in the throat'.[14]

Meanwhile, Thomas Elstob had played an increasingly important part in the running of the firm. This was reflected in his salary, which was £800 in 1844 then increased by £100 each year, except in 1847 when it jumped by £300. By 1853 he was receiving £1,800 and a sixteenth share of profits. It seems likely that he played the most important management role until his death in October 1866.

Poverty alongside Riches

The high salaries of top management contrasted sharply with the wages of the workers. In 1844 the typical wage of the framework knitters employed by Brettles – on their manager's own estimation – was between seven and fifteen shillings a week.[15] At most, therefore, the best workmen could earn up to £37 per year. Nor was this confined to Brettles. One Belper stockinger, after careful comparison of earnings, estimated that in 1844 the average earnings of the framework knitters in the town, clear of deductions, was 7/2d per week – less than £20 per annum.[16]

Nor was this just a Belper problem. The poverty of framework knitters and their families throughout the country was notorious in the early nineteenth century. Several Parliamentary enquiries were held to investigate the problems of the hosiery industry, of which the most exhaustive was undertaken in 1844–5, in the course of which the Belper companies were visited. William Wallis, who was the manager of the cotton department of George Brettle & Co. at the time, produced some figures for the Commissioner to show the year-by-year costs of making pairs of stockings and that both prices and wages were closely related to costs.[17] From these figures it appears that wages fell rapidly between between 1811 and 1819, recovered slightly in the early 1820s, fell again between 1825 and 1829, then stabilised in the 1830s and early 1840s. 'There has been no alteration, to my knowledge', stated Wallis in 1844, 'within the last twelve years.'[18]

On top of this, the stocking workers with 'company frames' had to pay 'frame rents' for the use of these, which was a running sore. Brettles' rates had long been fixed: they charged their workmen between 10d and a shilling a week according to the size or gauge of the frame. The managers regarded a fixed rent as fairer than charging a percentage on the work actually done, since that would, as Wallis put it, 'charge the hardworking man more than the idle one'.[19] But what appears to have been overlooked by management is that these frame rents were forming an increasing burden on the stockingers when their earnings were falling or the cost of living rising.

John Webster Hancock, manager of the Brettles silk department, was a fierce defender of the system of frame-renting. He was a man of strong individual opinions, and he did not hesitate to inflict them at length on the Commissioner on his 1844 visit to Belper. Hancock showed himself as having no great sympathies with the workers. He stated:

> There is sadly too much 'pretty prattle' to the working classes nowadays. It grows fulsome and they will get no good by it in the end. Their faults are many, and many of them are faults which they themselves could mend. I am no worshipper of the working classes. I have seen too much of them . . . Flatter them with fine words, tell them of great rights which are unjustly denied them, and which they could wield to perfection if they had them, and no men could be more attentive. You are an oracle; they will follow you through any political moonshine. But try to do them some good in their everyday business, and you are met on every side by knavery and tricks . . . The right of capital to gag and rob is not more universally acted upon than the right of poverty to cheat. Make it a rule to allow men their rent during sickness, and some rogues would scarcely ever be well. Our machinery would be worked for other people, and the workmen would pocket the rent. Every night's poaching, every drunken bout, every row and spree would be at our expense.[20]

Not a desirable boss, perhaps! But he was also scathing of capitalism:

> 'The main source of the evils facing the trade is the competitive system. All business now is war. We have left off in Europe, at least, the musket and the bayonet, and have taken to a sort of thuggery in the streets. Look where you will, they are all at it, stifling one another.'[21]

It would be interesting to know what the Brettle brothers thought of their Belper manager's outspoken views. Interestingly, the 1845 report said that Brettles employed two thousand hand frames on cotton hosiery, spread over the neighbouring villages for twenty miles around, in shops of between two to ten frames.

The poverty of hand-frame workers was a long-standing problem that Brettles inherited rather than created. An interesting 'talk on Belper' in 1901 (author unknown, but stored in St John's Chapel) states:

> In olden times, the old hand frame could be heard in this town and in the villages and hamlets around, with its well-known 'z-z-z-gigglle-a-gog-gog'. Wherever you hear that music, you could hear poverty. One man who had done it all his life told me, 'Stockinin is the poorest trade in the world. Many a thousand men has worked at it all their lives, never get above six or seven shillins a wick. Some as done rather better at the best sorts o work. But its bin a poor job for me, aw can assure yo. Need to pay for frame rent, for standing room, cost of needles, and light and life itself.'

The Royal Commission had started a long process, which would lead eventually to frame rents being abolished throughout the UK, but this prospect of lost revenue motivated management to recover it in other ways, to 'rein in' the frames for greater control, and to look for ways to centralise production and gain the economies of scale. As is so often the case in capitalist progress, a small victory gained for the workers, in this case home-based handloom workers, would be offset by the loss of their independence and autonomy in the long term.

New Fashions

Certainly the competition amongst hosiery manufacturers was intense, and market pressures from the late 1830s had forced them to trim costs – including labour – to the bone. Changes in fashion can be crucial for the textile trades. Up to 1837, as Hancock stated, 'middle class ladies including the wives and daughters of the better class of shopkeepers, manufacturers and professional men, were large consumers of silk stockings'. Thereafter, the demand fell off sharply, and depression rapidly struck the framework knitters. In the early 1840s Brettles were forced to set many of them to the making of woollen and thread gloves.[22]

Chevening had experienced a revival as the simple Regency style went out of fashion and the more elaborate wardrobes of the Victorians came into vogue. It had become the fashion to wear embroidered lisle, cashmere, cotton or silk stockings beneath the voluminous petticoats of the time. Indeed, the stockings worn by Queen Victoria on her Coronation day came from Brettles, and the firm subsequently added increasingly to its range of patterns and designs offered.

But the finest quality of silk stockings came to be less in demand with both ladies and gentlemen. The former were taking to long dresses, and the latter to trousers and boots. As Victorian practice succeeded Regency style, ladies were not showing off as much leg, and did not feel the need for the top-quality and more expensive stockings, which were now seen as impractical.

The new thinking was set out in 1844 by John Withers Taylor, the manager of Ward Sturt & Sharp's silk department:

> The moment a lady got a pair of good stockings on, if it was a dusty day they would not be seen for the dust covering them, and if it was a wet day they would be all over mud so that there would be no inducement for any lady to put on a pair of well-fashioned stockings. The gentlemen, on the other side, have taken to wearing boots

almost universally, and they want nothing under the boot of a fine kind. It does not matter to them how the stocking is made, if it will wear as well. All these things have a tendency to drive the manufacture into a lower grade altogether, for an article that is purely invisible in the wearing.[23]

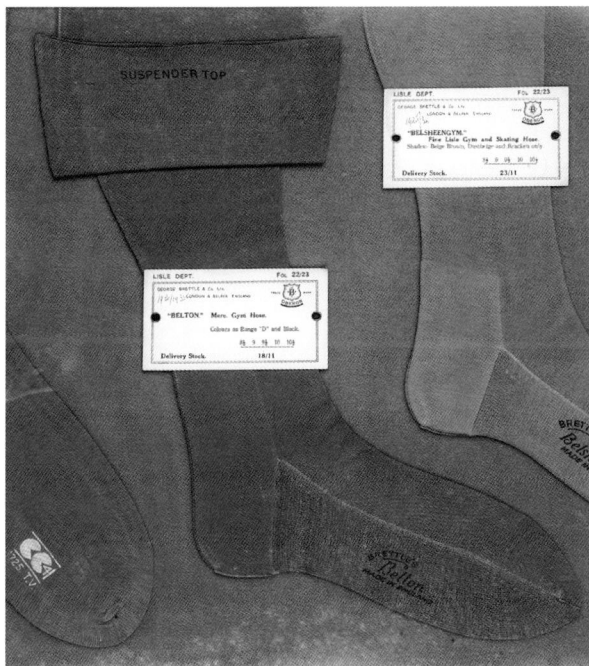

Left: 'Lisle Stockings' and **below** 'Prices of Socks, 1856' (Photographer : Nick Lockett).

GEORGE BRETTLE & CO.,
119, WOOD STREET, LONDON.

MANUFACTORY, BELPER, DERBYSHIRE.

1856 to 2 Marl 1857

PRICES OF SOCKS.

COTTON	1	2	3	4	5	6	7	8	9	10	WORSTED	1	2	3	4	5	6	7	8	9	10
F. White	0	10	1 4	1 10	2 4	2 10	3 4	3 10	4 4	4 10	Wt., Blk., Slate, Sorted & Grey	2 2	2 8	3 2	3 8	4 2	4 8	5 2	5 8	6 2	
Fine	1 0	1 6	2 0	2 6	3 0	3 6	4 0	4 6	5 0		Best Wt. Bk., Slate, Sorted & Grey	2 8	3 2	3 8	4 2	4 8	5 2	5 8	6 2	6 8	
Best Fine	1 6	2 0	2 6	3 0	3 6	4 0	4 6	5 0	5 6		Scarlet	2 4	2 10	3 4	3 10	4 4	4 10	5 4	5 10	6 4	
Super	1 11	2 5	2 11	3 5	3 11	4 5	4 11	5 5	5 11		Best Scarlet	2 10	3 4	3 10	4 4	4 10	5 4	5 10	6 4	6 10	
Fine Bleached	1 1	1 7	2 1	2 7	3 1	3 7	4 1	4 7	5 1		Best 3 Threads Sorted	4 3	4 9	5 3	5 9	6 3	6 9	7 3	7 9	8 3	
Super ditto																					

George Brettle II

The death of Elstob in 1866 and Edward Brettle the following year left George Henry Brettle as the only remaining partner and now in sole charge of the firm which already bore his name. Whilst continuing to take an active interest in the business, like his brothers he too had set himself up with a country seat. From about 1864 he had lived at Mongewell House in Oxfordshire, on the Thames just a mile downstream from Wallingford. Surrounded by 'extensive and well-arranged grounds' of some eighty acres, the house was formerly the southern seat of the Bishop of Durham.[24]

At that time, the firm consisted of five departments, each dealing in quite a range of goods:

- **Hosiery** – cotton hose and half-hose, silk and spun, lisle thread plain and lace, Balbriggan hose, socks, woollen and merino hose, shirts and pants, underclothing.

- **Fancy Hosiery** – knitted polkas, gaiters, boots, caps, hair nets, etc.

- **Gloves** – kid, silk, lisle, thread, cashmere, mitts, etc.

- **Haberdashery** – fringes, trimmings, braces, purses, umbrellas, carpet bags, shirts, neck ties.

- **Flannels** – real and imitation Welsh, Lancashire and Saxony, blankets and serges, carpets, rugs.

The majority of these items were bought in, so the commercial side of the firm in London continued to be considerably greater than the manufacturing side at Belper.[25]

George's takeover of the ownership and top management of the firm was not the easiest of times, and before the end of the year, recognising his responsibilities but feeling unable to commit to lone management, he brought four of the firm's senior employees into the partnership. These were William Smithyman Bean, Parmenas Martin Burgess, George Dickson and Frederic William Sharp. Bean had been in the firm since 1829, Sharp since 1835, Dickson since 1838 and Burgess since 1840.

Above: View of Brettles Mill and surroundings. Postcard Picture taken by Mrs Stone, Nether Heage, 1900s.

Towards Mass Production

The main company achievement of this period was the late progression to full factory production. The domestic system had hung on as it suited both sides of the industry, for it enabled convenient family involvement, maximised use of the frames and output, and had the advantages of today's remote and flexible working. That apart, management had long believed that it was or would be very difficult to harness steam power or water power for centralised hosiery production. 'One great argument against our introducing the factory system', said one of the Wards managers in 1844, 'is that we cannot find any means of employing steam power.'[26] For Brettles, John W. Hancock had gone further: 'Stockings cannot be made by power, and I believe they never will be.'[27]

But the need to attain the economies of scale would find its own solution. The first successful factory producing hosiery had been erected in 1851 by the Nottingham firm of Hine & Mundella. Opening in the same year that the Great Exhibition at Crystal Palace was focusing attention on industrial progress, it excited much attention.[28] But most hosiers decided to 'wait and see'.

The breakthrough nationally came in the 1860s through William Cotton, the best-known name of those involved in the mechanisation of hosiery, who then invented the most satisfactory form of rotary frame, the original 'Cotton's Patent'. The rights to this were bought by Hine & Mundella, who extended their factory accordingly in 1866, and later also by Morleys of Nottingham.

But already, small moves towards factory production had been started in some places, including Belper. Here the way was led by Wards, who had introduced steam power into their dyeing and bleaching works by 1846. Their 'extensive' finishing establishment was situated opposite their warehouse on the Derby Road, immediately to the south of Brettles' warehouse, and there they employed a 40 hp steam engine.[29] Brettles products at that time were still being sent to specialist dyers and bleachers in Nottinghamshire. In 1849 the Wards warehouse was destroyed by fire, but it was rebuilt the following year, and with it a factory containing 30 ordinary hosiery frames, 36 circular machines and six or eight described as 'very wide ones that go by steam power'.[30]

Brettles appear to have started their first real factory at about the same time. John Ross, manager of the firm much later, in the 1930s, did his own research and concluded that 'about 1850, accommodation was provided for both hand-frames and power rotary frames in factory premises'.[31] It is not possible to trace his sources, but in 1873 it was discovered that 'the Factory' (which was described as 'fire-proof') and 'the Factory Frames' were not covered by insurance as was the warehouse. In 1874 there was reference to 'the Factory' having been 'kept going constantly' during the previous two years.[32] So, at the latest, it was up and running by 1872.

The outside hand looms were brought into the factory. In the early days of no gas or electricity, night work and anything 'after dusk' was a problem. Brettles' solution was to hang a glass bowl of water, coloured light blue, beside a machine, and then put a lighted candle behind it. The bowl refracted the light right along the machine, giving a glow which resembled daylight.[33]

But the coming of electricity enabled the scaling up of production and of exports. Related to this, in 1870, Charles Cotton, brother to the better-known William Cotton, and who was also a hosiery machine builder, invented an improved rotary knitting machine.[34] Brettles became interested in this. On 3rd May 1871 Isaac Hanson, by now the Belper manager, wrote to the partners in London about it:

> In regard to the new Patent Frame, Parker and I saw it yesterday and have an idea of its making as valuable a machine as Morleys & Mundella's patent . . . In some points it is superior . . . There are several Nottingham people after it, but the man agrees to hold it open for GB & Co. until Tuesday next. He wants to come and install it in our shop at £2 per week, would be finished in about a month, and would then sell it to us for £80, and would sell the patent for £250 . . .

This was agreed, and Brettles bought the patent in order 'for them to either build, work or vend the said machine'.[35] They then developed the improved methods it brought to the production of fashioned wool, mercerised lisle and pure silk stockings. Sales and customers grew and the firm made a serious start with exporting. All this appears to have been achieved during the years of George Henry Brettle's leadership and that of his four chosen co-partners.

But just four years after this team was fielded, it was left captainless. George Henry Brettle became seriously ill late in 1871, and on 29th January 1872 he died, aged just 52. One of his partners wrote of 'his shattered constitution' that 'in trying to remedy the evils of one disease it affected another, and so the poor man died of dropsy and diseased liver'. He was buried in a simple grave in the grounds of the old Norman church at Mongewell, where his brother Edward was also buried. But both brothers' names (though not Alfred) appear under that of their father on his monument in St Peter's Church at Belper, close to the altar. Constructed by Sir Richard Westmacott, and described by Pevsner as 'of the best workmanship', it portrays a languishing Grecian female.[36]

Thus the business had survived and grown under George Brettle's sons, but had been overtaken by some others. Within a decade of George Brettle's death in 1835, the claim to be 'the most extensive hosiers in the kingdom' could no longer be made, as the Wards expanded their manufacturing capacity and outstripped them for the next sixty years. Also, by mid century the claim to be the largest firm of merchant hosiers had been lost to I. & R. Morley, whose London warehouse was rebuilt on a grand scale in 1850.[37] But survive they did – and survive well.

Opposite: Brettles Memorial, St Peter's Church, to George Henry Brettle and Edward Brettle
(Photographer: Nick Lockett).

IN MEMORY OF

GEORGE BRETTLE. ESQUIRE

OF RALEIGH LODGE. BRIXTON HILL:

BORN 1ST JANUARY 1778. DIED 18TH OCTOBER 1835.

ALSO OF **EDWARD**. ELDEST SON OF THE ABOVE:

DIED 20TH MAY 1867. AGED 48 YEARS.

ALSO OF **GEORGE HENRY BRETTLE. ESQRE**,

OF MONGEWELL HOUSE:

SECOND SON OF THE ABOVE DIED 29TH JANY 1872

IN HIS 52ND YEAR.

4. THE COMING OF THE TWYFORDS

Like both his brothers, George Henry Brettle left no sons, and so there was a good deal of concern about the future of the firm. However, as George Dickson, one of the four remaining partners, wrote to a customer in March 1872, 'It was Mr Brettle's dying wish that dear old Wood Street should be protected . . . I am happy to tell you that arrangements are being made that the business will be continuing as before, as the widow has been left sole executor . . .' Apart from a few personal bequests to servants, George Brettle left all his property to his wife, Helen.[1]

In June 1872 Helen signed a new partnership agreement with her husband's junior partners, Bean, Burgess, Dickson and Sharp. She was to have 'paramount control' of the business, while its management was to be undertaken by the others, with George Dickson as 'the financial partner' having 'the principal and chief management'. The partners were to have a larger share in the firm's profits than they had previously: each was to receive a sixth of the profits, and Helen Brettle the remaining third. George Dickson said the partners thought the new agreement 'a very fair and liberal paper'. It was arranged to have 'a mahogany box' in which to send the accounts to Mrs Brettle for her periodic perusal, and this arrangement continued throughout the rest of her life.

In April 1873, fifteen months after she had been widowed, Helen Brettle found a new husband. She married a Colonel Henry Robert Twyford. He had been an officer in the army, a Captain in the 36th Regiment of Foot Soldiers, and from 1864 a Lieutenant Colonel in the 2nd Administrative Battalion of the Hampshire Rifle Volunteers.[2] The Twyfords lived at Trotton, a village in Sussex between Midhurst and the Hampshire border, where they were lords of the manor.[3]

When Helen Brettle became Mrs Twyford, it was agreed that she would carry on the business of George Brettle & Co. as 'femme sole', independently of her husband. She sold Mongewell House in Oxfordshire, and they set up home together at Bournemouth.

Weathering the Great Depression

The 1870s were the decade which came to be perceived as the 'Great Depression' compared with the previous Victorian prosperity. It was a tough time for the business, and for the hosiery trade as a whole, and this was reflected in George Dickson's reports from Wood Street to Helen Twyford. In April 1874 he wrote that trade was 'very far from satisfactory', and later that year that 'business is very indifferent and backward, that is, people will put off their purchases to the very latest time'.

After a slight improvement in 1875 and 1876, he wrote in 1877 that trade was 'very bad indeed', and noted that in terms of payments the firm was receiving 'numerous applications for accommodation' from its customers, and that he had 'never felt nor known such internal anxiety regarding business'.

Helen Twyford expressed her disappointment at that year's accounts:

> The expenses sweep away the bulk of the profits, I might almost say the whole. Belper again allowed to languish, its production getting lower year by year whilst we buy from other manufacturers what we are capable of producing ourselves. Unless some very great change in the result of our trading takes place, there is no inducement to me to continue the house as far as I am concerned.

Solemn words, but no immediate solution was at hand. In 1879 again, Dickson said trade was simply 'deplorable'.[4]

Dickson recognised that part of the problem was German competition. From the 1860s the textile area of Chemnitz had been quick to adopt the latest technology and machinery.[5] And in 1876 Dickson was especially concerned to hear that the German manufacturers had lowered their wages by 10 per cent, making them lower even than those in England and their prices consequently more competitive.

Besides this, there were internal problems in the company. Frame rents had been finally abolished by Act of Parliament in 1874, but discontent over rates of pay continued, and in 1876 the firm had to face its first major strike of factory employees. However, damage was mitigated by the large stocks and slowness of trade. 'I know it is painful for you and us to see the factory steam-power still,' wrote Dickson to Isaac Hanson, the Belper manager, 'but it could not occur at a time more suitable for us.' Were it not for the strike, he pointed out, the factory would only 'be working for the uncertainty of next year's trade'.[6] The firm were saved the expense of paying wages at a time when more output was not needed. It was well timed; in terms of production, it was expedient to stand still.

The firm received expressions of sympathy from other manufacturers, and Wards offered their help, placing their machinery and premises at Brettles' disposal. Caught in the same slump themselves and with spare capacity, they could no doubt well afford to do so! However, it does suggest that whatever acrimony there may have been between the two Belper firms was now a thing of the past.

Soon after, George Brettle & Co. lost three of its partners. In May 1877 William Smithyman Bean died, after 46 years with the firm. In the same year Frederic William Sharp retired, having reached his personal goal of having accumulated capital of £20,000. Then in October 1879 Parmenas Martin Burgess resigned, after 39 years with the firm, leaving George Dickson as the only working partner. The following year, Helen Twyford brought two more senior employees into the partnership. They were Isaac Hanson, Belper factory manager since 1864, and John Scott, cotton department manager in London. At the same time, in a new will she left the business to her husband, expressing her 'wish and intention . . . that my said husband carry on the same for his own benefit after my decease'.[7]

At the end of 1880 George Dickson compiled comparative figures for the previous forty years. These have not survived, but remarkably, despite the problems described, he said in summary that the sales for 1871–80 showed a total increase of £155,837 over those for 1861–70, and of £312,203 over those for 1841–50. Furthermore, early in the depression the firm had invested in its future. In 1874, improvements to the factory buildings and to the steam engine had been undertaken, and new frames put in. A new access road was made at the back of the factory 'for the purpose of carrying coals, timber and boilers or other heavy machinery'.

Colonel Twyford's Takeover

In the general election of 1880, Colonel Twyford stood as the Conservative candidate for Newport on the Isle of Wight, and was only narrowly defeated.[8] In 1881 Helen Twyford's health began to fail and, despite periods of convalescence at Brighton and Hastings, she died in November 1882. Her nominal control of her first husband's firm had lasted ten years.

Though a retired soldier with no experience of hosiery or any other trade, Colonel

Twyford shouldered his new responsibilities and met with his wife's junior partners on 24th November 1882, just 22 days after her death. Two days later, George Dickson, who in recent years had effectively become the head of the business, suddenly died. In the new articles of partnership that took effect from December 1883, he was replaced by John Scott in 'the general supervision of the London business', and, as a third junior partner, in came John Henry Mallard, manager of the worsted department. Twyford himself was to have 'paramount control', but 'shall be at liberty to absence himself therefrom or employ himself therein at his own will and pleasure'.[9]

In 1883, a year after his first wife's death, Twyford married Lady Duke, née Jane Amelia Bennett, widow of Sir James Duke, first baronet, who had died in 1873.[10] The new couple had houses in London at Queen's Gate, South Kensington, later in Cadogan Square, and also at Hove.

The main commercial change taking place in the last quarter of the nineteenth century was that an increasing proportion of the firm's output took the form of knitted underwear rather than stockings. Also, whilst many established customers continued to visit the Wood Street premises to place their orders (where a wine room was maintained for their entertainment), another feature of the period was the rise of the commercial traveller. This change was necessitated by the increasing number of customers outside the London market, and was facilitated by the growing rail network during the second half of the century. It went hand-in-hand with changes in the nature of the customer base, with the evolution of many retail drapers into department stores. Peter Robinson, Swan & Edgar, Debenham & Freebody, Marshall & Snelgrove, Shoolbreds, Whiteleys and Barkers were all well-known names of the time, who were supplied by George Brettle & Co.

Isaac Hanson continued as partner and as Belper factory manager, and also became a JP and a leading figure in many community activities. He lived at Chevin Mount, the house he had built for himself overlooking the factory on a hill on the other side of the Derwent, until his death in 1911.

Right: 'Chevin Mount, Manager Isaac Hanson's house on Chevin ridge.' (Courtesy of Ray Marjoram and Belper Historical Society).

Cosy Consolidation

All indicators are that the 1880s and 90s were better years for Brettles than the 1870s had been. The closing years of the nineteenth century, and indeed the first decade of the twentieth century, saw the business strong and profitable, but not marked by innovation or dramatic growth. Rather it took pride in having become a long-established respected business, valued by all who dealt with it, maintaining time-honoured practices, but perhaps resting rather complacently on its laurels. Further real growth and innovation awaited the arrival of another Twyford, and, ironically, the First World War.

There is ample testimony from employees and customers alike to their fondness for 'dear old Wood Street', as George Brettle had called it. One customer who visited regularly from 1866 described it as 'one of the most charming warehouses in the city'.[11] For the live-in employees, there was a camaraderie that grew in the bedrooms (generally with four beds) and the common rooms above the warehouse and offices. There had been established since 1850 a library, a debating society, the 'Oberon' cricket and football clubs (see Chapter 8).[12] Over these years, many spoke of their enjoyment of the 'larking and ragging', the talking after lights-out, the sports matches, the club dinners and suppers, the trips to Gilbert & Sullivan operettas and other attractions.

One letter that shows how well the employees were looked after was written by a newly-employed youngster to his aunt:

> I got paid today as they always pay monthly . . . The food is jolly good, the dinner from the joint, served just like it is in a restaurant at 2/6 per luncheon. The meat is carved off and brought to us by a waiter. We can have hot meat which is roasted, or we can have cold meat, ham, beef, tongue or lamb, with salad or pickles or mint sauce. The waiter then hands us a dish of potatoes to help ourselves from, then the greens, then brings us mustard, salt, pickles, salad or whatever we want, then bread, and finally pours us out a glass of water or ale or stout, whichever we prefer. You should see the fellows shift the beer, pints of it, and they can have as much as they like, as we can with everything. We can have two or three helpings of meat if we like. Sometimes we have fruit or custard, and afterwards cheese . . .[13]

Working a Hand frame, Silk Hosiery, June 1923.

Old Neddy Smith working his hand frame.

There is evidence of considerable employee loyalty at both London and Belper. The best example of this is Edward 'Old Neddy' Smith of Belper, who spent 87 years working for Brettles! He had begun work on his father's hand-loom at the age of ten in 1827, and continued to knit on it for the rest of his life. His early adulthood was spent very much under the shadow of his dominant father, who received the wages and passed nothing on to his son until the age of 28, when Ned was granted just one shilling a week because he was caught stealing his father's tobacco. The old man thrashed him for this, to which Ned is reported to have said: 'Make it a good 'un, it's the last you'll ever gie me, it'll be your turn next.' Soon after this he at last became a Brettles wage earner in his own right. Well over sixty years later, at the age of 96, he was indignant at being offered retirement with a generous pension, and retorted: 'If they couldna find me more work, I'll get another job.' He continued working until three weeks before his death at the age of 97 in January 1914. It was said that he had never seen the sea, and not even been to Derby until he was in his nineties.[14]

The early years of the new century saw the loss of all of the 'junior' partners. In 1901 Isaac Hanson retired after his long reign over the Belper factory. Scott died on the last day of 1903 and Mallard in August 1904. Thereafter, Henry Robert Twyford was the sole partner in the business until his death in 1913. His second wife had died in 1900. He retained an active part in management, and whilst spending more time at London, he maintained a house at Belper, 'Sunny Bank', and spent some time there every summer. In Derbyshire he was known as 'a very generous subscriber to local institutions and charities, besides being a staunch supporter of the Conservative cause'.[15]

Sunny Bank House, Twyford's second home in Belper.

St Peter's Church Belper.

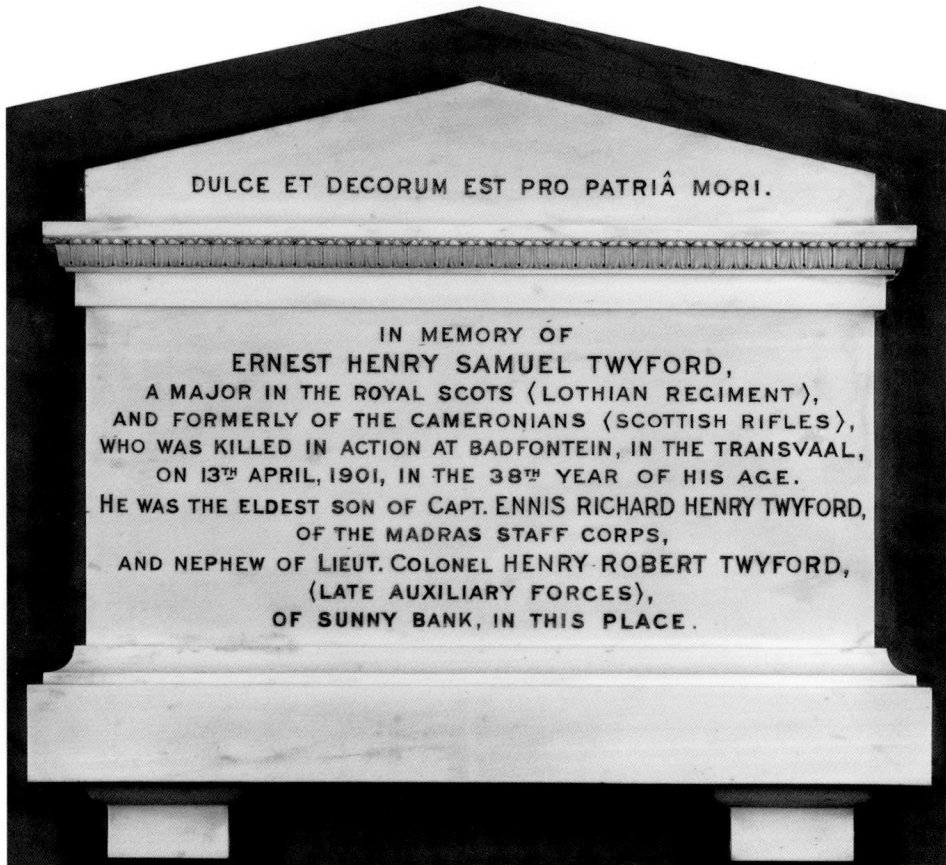

DULCE ET DECORUM EST PRO PATRIÂ MORI.

IN MEMORY OF
ERNEST HENRY SAMUEL TWYFORD,
A MAJOR IN THE ROYAL SCOTS (LOTHIAN REGIMENT),
AND FORMERLY OF THE CAMERONIANS (SCOTTISH RIFLES),
WHO WAS KILLED IN ACTION AT BADFONTEIN, IN THE TRANSVAAL,
ON 13TH APRIL, 1901, IN THE 38TH YEAR OF HIS AGE.
HE WAS THE ELDEST SON OF CAPT. ENNIS RICHARD HENRY TWYFORD,
OF THE MADRAS STAFF CORPS,
AND NEPHEW OF LIEUT. COLONEL HENRY ROBERT TWYFORD,
(LATE AUXILIARY FORCES),
OF SUNNY BANK, IN THIS PLACE.

Twyford Memorial, St. Peters Church, to Ernest Henry Twyford (1863–1901) son of Ennis Richard Henry Twyford, brother of Henry Robert Twyford, killed in Boer War. (Photographer : Nick Lockett)

5. FROM PARTNERSHIP TO COMPANY

Old Colonel Twyford died in April 1913, leaving no children by either of his marriages, just a stepson by his second, Sir James Duke, second baronet, who was never concerned in the firm. He left the business equally to his nephews Lionel Thomas Campbell Twyford and Harry Edward Augustus Twyford, the sons of his late brothers.[1]

The following month, the report of the firm's accountants, Josolyne Miles & Co., drew attention to a number of faults in the way the firm's business was conducted. They commented on the unnecessarily high stock levels, the slow turnover of stock, the heavy travelling expenses of travellers, the relatively high salaries of some, and the inadequate system of accounts.[2] These pressing issues were addressed by the two Twyfords; for example, they decided to pay the travellers by a combination of salary and commission, thus introducing a 'productivity' incentive. Other changes followed, some of them small, but together indicating that progress was afoot. In late June it was decided to replace the three horse vans with a one-ton motor van. In October the North London 'horse brougham' was replaced by a motor car. The firm was being dragged into the twentieth century.

In January 1914 the business was incorporated as a private limited company, George Brettle & Co. Ltd, which of course required it to produce proper annual accounts. Lionel Twyford, as the elder brother, became Chairman of the new company, but almost immediately was recalled to the active list as a Brigadier General, and then sent to war. So Harry was the active director from the start.

The same month, at Belper, 'Old Neddy' Smith died, the last surviving man to remember George Brettle senior. A link with the past was broken; it was the end of an era, and the start of a new one.

In March 1915 Alfred Murrell Gibson became the third director. He had served the firm since joining it in 1889 at the age of 17, first in the underwear department, then as West End representative from 1906. He was promoted to Buyer in 1913, to General Manager in 1914, and to Director in 1915.

The Fortunes of War

After war broke out in 1914, a number of workers signed up and joined the armed forces, including two who were later to become directors. H.O. Randall was already in the London Rifle Brigade Territorials and was quickly mobilised; he served with them and later with the RAMC in Egypt and Palestine. W.H. Inch served with the Kensington Battalion of the London Rifles and in the Machine Gun Corps, saw active service in France, where he was wounded, and later became a Second Lieutenant in the Kings Royal Rifles.[3]

However, company investment continued. In 1915 a new type of machinery was introduced into the factory besides the established 'Cotton's patents' – circular web machines, which cut underwear, and ribbed knitting and seamless hose began to be used. The factory was producing underwear and stockings in cotton, silk and wool, besides a quantity of knickers, ties and gloves.

The First World War was a good period for Brettles. From a modest £38,090 in 1914, their sales multiplied nearly five times to £176,062 in 1918. Army orders for underwear and stockings constituted a high proportion of this increase in production. But there was another factor. In 1915, the warehouse of Ward Sturt & Sharp in London was bombed by a Zeppelin and seriously damaged by fire, which in retrospect marked the beginning of the end for that partnership business. From this point on, their Belper building was used only as a warehouse, to accommodate the stocks from London. Their manufacturing ceased and was transferred over the road to Brettles, who then became Wards' main supplier. Brettles could not have possibly known that there would be another world war in a little over twenty years' time, in which they would suffer the same setback in the Blitz, but survive it.

After the War

At the end of the war it was decided to build an extension to the factory. To this end in 1919 a further field behind the factory was purchased from G.H. Strutt, and the extension built and equipped with new plant. In the same year, William Miller Bowness was appointed manager of the Belper factory. Most of his experience had been outside the company: he had worked his way up through a Mansfield hosiery factory, had been a traveller and had worked for a London shipping house. One of his first actions as Manager was to introduce double shift working. The increased production was creating a bottleneck in the finishing stages, so he also rented a large building in Wirksworth, north-west of Belper, to provide extra accommodation and labour for linking, seaming and other such operations. Output crossed the £200,000 line in 1919 and reached £264,391 in 1920, a striking difference from the £38,090 of just six years earlier.

Above: Brettles Seaming Room, Wirksworth, probably 1930s and below Mr. Rayford, Head of the Counting House (later Company Secretary) at his desk, 1910.

In 1920, soon after his return from war, Lionel Twyford died, and Harry succeeded to the Chairmanship of the company; he was to oversee its growth and to remain in charge of it right through until its acquisition by Courtaulds in 1964. Also in 1920, Frank John Rayson was made a director. Rayson had joined the firm in 1875 and risen to be Chief Clerk, and, after 1905, 'Head of the Counting House'. Since the company had been formed in 1915, he had been its Secretary.

In 1925, Harry Twyford's son Richard was brought onto the board. Born in 1900, Dick Twyford had spent his earliest years in his mother's native Australia, then moving to Penang and to New Zealand. After coming to the UK, he spent some time with a firm of machine makers in Nottingham before joining the Wood Street staff in 1923, becoming Manager of the Claims department.[4]

In the firm's manufacturing processes, working on a large scale had become the norm. Mary Smedley records that the last local independent home-based framework knitter had finished working his own frame at Bargate in 1913.[5] The employed hand-loom workers and their looms had been brought in-house some years previously, and had no doubt found the transition difficult. But by this time most of them had retired and their looms had been scrapped. A small number of hand frames were kept at the factory up to the mid 1930s to meet the occasional special orders, such as swimsuits for oriental royalty and their harems, and very high-quality hose for the super-rich. One of the last special orders to be produced this way was some silk half-hose for Primo Carnera, the giant Italian heavyweight boxer. Otherwise it was mass production by powered machinery. The same changes had taken place throughout the textile industries, and Brettles was by no means the last to complete them.

Through Boom and Slump

During the inter-war period, the old staple industries were hard hit, especially as the bottom was falling out of the export market. Meanwhile some newer industries that were orientated to home demand for consumer goods had a high growth rate. While historically belonging to the first of these categories, apart from small slumps in the early 1920s and 30s the overall experience of the hosiery industry was one of growth. Whilst the general cotton and woollen industries declined, numbers employed in hosiery as a whole rose from under 100,000 in the early 1920s to more than 133,000 in the late 1930s. Total production of stockings increased from 25,400,000 dozens in 1924 to 35,981,000 in 1937, and of underwear from 6,514,000 dozens to 12,789,000.[6]

Brettles shared in the prosperity of the hosiery industry. Record profits were made between 1917 and 1919, and a high proportion of these were ploughed back into the firm – £95,966 in 1917, £142,672 in 1918, and £141,119 in 1919. At the height of the firm's fortunes, there were proposals for it to acquire John Smedley Ltd, an old-established high-quality hosiery manufacturer at Lee Bridge, north-east of Belper. Draft heads of agreement were drawn up, but, for reasons unknown, these proposals were not pursued. However, it is interesting that a few years later Brettles were selling some Smedley lines: 'Star Seat' ladies' knickers and 'Jay Finish' silk and wool trunk drawers.

Over the inter-war period as a whole, Brettles' output of manufactured goods rose. Back in 1914, production at Belper had provided only a seventeenth of the total goods sold by the firm in London. By 1921 it accounted for almost a fifth of total sales, and by the late 1920s about a quarter, a level that was maintained throughout the 1930s.

But it was not all progress. The boom of 1917–19 was followed by a short slump, which turned a high profit of £141,119 into a loss of £103,836 in 1920, and a smaller loss of £15,472 in 1921, whilst sales fell from a peak of one and three quarter million in 1920 to just a little over a million the following year. The firm was forced to borrow from the National Provincial Bank, who were asked to provide an overdraft facility of £120,000 in March 1920, increased to £165,000 in August. In 1922, debentures worth £35,000 were reissued to nominees of the bank as security for their loans.[7]

Overall productivity increases were considered necessary to rectify the situation. Thus in 1923 it was decided to require all London departments to make a gross profit of 16 per cent per annum. Some failed to do so, and as a consequence Haberdashery (the smallest department) was closed down in 1924 and the Bandanna department in 1927. At this time the largest departments were the Lisle (accounting for a quarter of sales) and Silk departments, and these were able to meet their targets. The firm's tough measures in response to the slump appear to have proved successful.

The Lisle department accounted for a sixth of sales in 1920 and about a quarter from 1927. The main products in this category were the various ladies' fully fashioned stockings, made at Belper out of fine mercerised cotton, and sold under the names of 'Silkestia' and 'Lustrinia' in a range of colours, from black to flesh and from purple and lilac to sky blue. 'Silkestia' were plain and unpatterned; 'Lustrinia' had a small design on the side known as 'self clox'. The department also handled a growing quantity of artificial silk hose such as 'Gleam'.

Big Factory Photo Session, June 1923

Manufacturing

Finishing department, Fashioned Underwear, June 1923.

Circular Web machines, June 1923.

Stocking Frame making, June 1923.

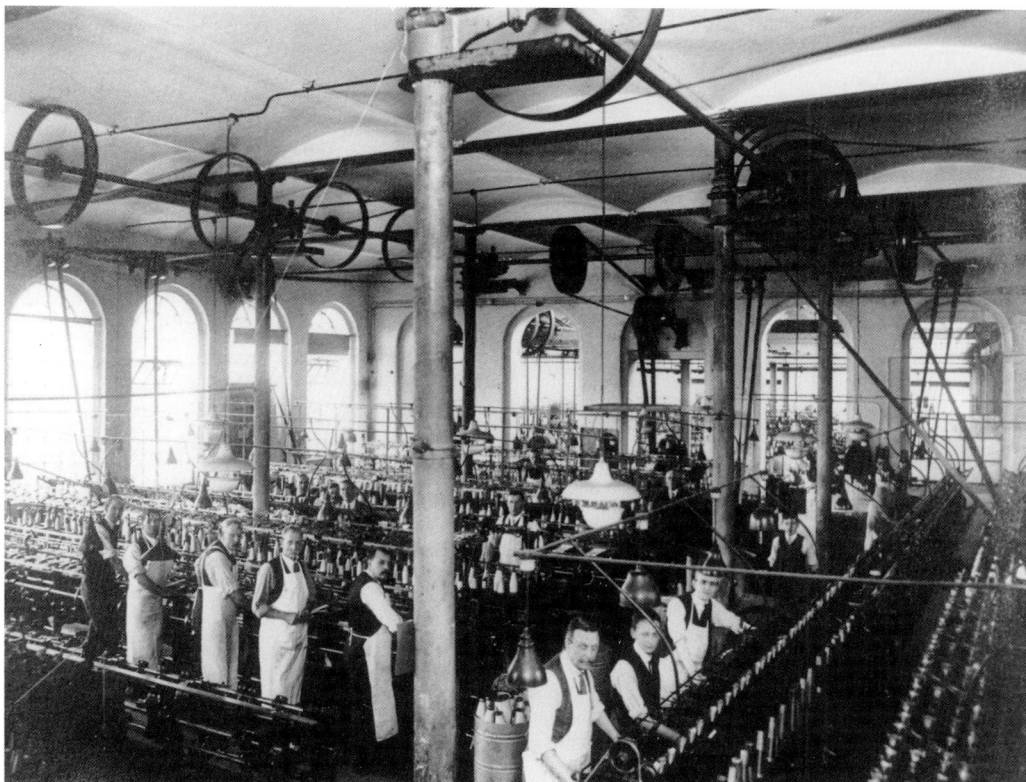

Cotton Frames for Fashion Hosiery.

Seaming Hose, June 1923.

Ribbed Underwear, making up, June 1923.

Ribbed Underwear department, June 1923.

Packing into boxes, June 1923.

The 'Pairing' process, June 1923.

'Boarding' – stretching hosiery of preformed shades, June 1923.

Corner of Winding Room, June 1923.

Services

Brettles Textile Laboratory.

Printing Department.

Mechanics Shop.

General Office, June 1923.

Factory Garage, cars & drivers, 1920s.

Direct Current Generators, June 1923.

Canteen and Parties

Canteen Kitchens, 1920s.

Brettles Childrens Christmas Party, 1929.

Brettles Childrens Christmas Party, 1929.

Framework Knitters Christmas meal, 17th December 1932.

Machine Builders

In 1928, the firm began making its own machines, which was most unusual for a hosiery manufacturer. The complex machines capable of knitting several garments at once, which the industry used in the 1920s, were normally built by specialist engineering firms, the most important being that established by William Cotton in the 1870s. W.M. Bowness, the Belper manager, travelled to the United States and Germany on the firm's behalf to investigate best-practice technology, and concluded that German machines were unsuitable and that British firms would take over a year to supply. He decided that the development would be done in-house and that he would directly supervise it. The mechanics' shop was consequently extended and the firm's engineer, Ron Sheppard, was set to designing and building the machines. By the end of 1928, the long 39-gauge full-fashioned machine, with variable speed motor and specially designed control gear, was ready to knit sixteen garments at once.

In the same year, large additions were made to the factory buildings; a new extension, costing £14,000, covered 36,000 square feet and contained over twenty of the latest full-fashion machines. On 21st December 1928 there was a grand party held to celebrate the opening of the factory extension, attended by over a thousand employees and guests. The highlight of the evening was the starting up by Mrs Twyford of the first machine for making fully fashioned hose that had been built on the premises by Brettles' own workers. This landmark occasion led Bowness to proclaim that the event was 'the greatest day in the history of the company'. Harry Twyford claimed that productivity per worker had risen 73 per cent since 1913 and that if duties on raw silk imports were removed he would immediately give orders for another extension and find employment for 300 to 400 more.[8]

Several more machines were in the process of construction at the time. In fact, Bowness suggested there was no reason why the firm might not start making machines for other manufacturers, and for a time 'machine builders' was added to its letterhead. Five more machines were built over the next few years, but only for Brettles' own use. In 1932 Bowness brought in a German technical expert, Fritz Friedrich, to help with this work, and he was provided with a house in Derbyshire. But it was found that he had little idea of how to erect a hosiery machine, and after two years he was dismissed.

First fully-fashioned machine built by Brettles, December 1928.

Drawing of 119 Wood Street and Belper Mill, showing directors, managers & salesmen, 1929
(Photographer: Nick Lockett).

North side of Brettles Factory, Chapel Street, Belper, 1920s/30s.

Exit Ward Sturt & Sharp

In 1930, the once rival firm of Ward Sturt & Sharp ceased trading, perhaps an early victim of the 1930s recession. Its turnover in the 1920s had languished between £353,000 and £460,000, in 1929 they had made a net loss, and, facing a greater loss in 1930, the remaining partners, H. Leader Sturt and Wilfred L. Sturt, placed the firm in the hands of its creditors for its assets to be realised. Though there remained a £38,687 surplus of assets over liabilities, the firm was liquidated.[9]

And so it was that, nearly a century after George Brettle had been forced to give up the use of Wards' warehouse, his company had the opportunity to purchase it back. In the event they decided not to purchase the warehouse itself, but for the low price of £2,950 they did buy the Ward property on their own side of the Derby Road. On the site was the Dye House that Wards had built some years before, and this enabled Brettles to start their own dyeing, which had previously been done by outside dyers (they invested £15,000 in this over the next three years). Also included on the acquired site was the old framesmiths' shop which they had long rented from Wards; the sock department and most of the circular machinery were moved there, and it later became the 'Belnit' factory.

The main Wards building was acquired by Dalton & Co. and used as an oil refinery for some years. The 'Wards warehouse' building still stands today, as does the adjacent Brook Cottage, which was home to John Ward then to Benjamin Ward. Though empty and somewhat the worse for wear, it is now a listed structure.

It appears that many of Wards' employees were taken on. At the end of 1928 Brettles had been employing 800 people in Belper, but by the end of 1930 it was over a thousand. The firm was now easily the largest employer in Belper. At the height of its prosperity, it commenced publication of a magazine entitled *Yarns*, proudly subtitled 'The Magazine of the House of Brettle', with a shield marked 'B' and the Latin motto 'Labor Omnia Vincit': 'Hard Work Conquers All'. Thirteen issues were produced between 1929 and 1932, when publication ended as there was less good news to tell.

Right: Cleaning Wards Boiler following purchase, October 1933 – showing W. Spendlove, R. Blount, A. Parkin and others.

Below: Brettles Dye House.

View from Dyeworks Chimney top, about 1930.

Traction engine pulling Boiler, 30 tons, 30 ft. long, 8 ft.6 inch diameter.

Boiler arriving from Dukinfield, end view.

Roof top view from Brettles facing north.

New Factory Boilers in situ, Brettles Mill, Belper.

Through the Recession

It is clear that the company did suffer briefly from the recession of the early 1930s. One classic symptom of this was a freeze on recruitment. Whilst other firms around made redundancies, so that the numbers of unemployed grew, the worst that Brettles staff had to face was a resort to short-time working and consequent pay cut, which naturally brought some discontent. The message went out to staff that they were 'lucky to still have a job'. In the last 1932 issue of *Yarns*, one anonymous manager inserted a poem entitled 'Get On or Get Out':

> There's many a man can do your job
> As good or better than you.
> There's many a man to take your place
> And be glad of the offer too!
>
> If you want your job, get on with your job.
> If not, it's up to you
> To quit it now and so make room
> For a man more keen to do.
>
> Get on with your job or get out of your job,
> Which are you going to do?
> We can't waste time on slackers now,
> So choose – it's up to you.
>
> It's up to you to make of your job
> The best success you can.
> If you can't do that, it's up to you
> To give it to those who can!

At least they had that choice, unlike today, when most workers in such circumstances apparently have no choice at all! The same magazine carried a letter from 'Chairman Mr Alderman Twyford' saying:

> I am afraid many have been disappointed with 1932 who had hoped to have seen a revival of trade and better times. However, we must look forward, with our hearts full of hope that 1933 may be the turning point, and that trade will improve and with it bring prosperity to all of us.[10]

But his hopes for 1933 were premature, as it was another year or two before the firm would turn the corner.

It might be assumed from the foregoing that the company had been making heavy losses, but this was not the case. In fact the firm suffered much less in the 1930s slump than it had in that of the early 1920s. The rate of profit had fallen from 10 per cent in 1930 to 5 per cent, after which it rallied. Perhaps the London perception, and Harry's comments, had more to do with the state of the wholesale side.

In fact the internal accounts indicate that whilst the London side of the company was still making small losses until 1939, the Belper side was making decent profits again from 1934:[11]

Year:	1934	1935	1936	1937	1938
London	(2,214)	(2,930)	(87)	(2,047)	(3,679)
Belper	15,635	15,004	13,940	18,628	20,610

Perhaps this was a factor in an emergency management decision that would be made in 1941. Be that as it may, it is a familiar feature that, in times of recession, companies gain briefly from competitors who go out of business as some of their customers are picked up, which can mask the effect of the underlying economic circumstances. No doubt Brettles did this and it must have helped them ride the recession.

Left: Belper Carnival Hosiery Queen 1936: Brettles employee D. Sheldon.

Out with the Old

In August 1936, Deputy Factory Manager John Ross poignantly noted in his scrapbook: 'Wallis Walker and William Haslam pensioned off. These two men are the last of our hand-frame workers. So ends an old industry.' And after 1936, the only outworkers mentioned in the firm's books were cheveners, who embroidered designs onto stockings and socks, a local specialist occupation. Smedley records that there were still cheveners operating in Belper until the mid 1980s.[12]

On the London side, the early 1930s had seen the end of 'living in' at 119 Wood Street; the cosy paternalism enjoyed by generations of apprentices was over. The space was needed, and it became cheaper to pay employees to find digs than to keep up an elaborate domestic economy.

However, under Harry Twyford's direction, the firm had increased the other provisions made for its growing number of employees. The self-help Oberon Insurance Society – the 'Coffin Club' – founded in 1920, was replaced in 1928 by the introduction of life insurance and a pension for all employees from the age of 65 that was widely regarded as a model scheme.[13] Harry claimed that 'Brettles was the first firm in the textile trade to have a staff pension insurance scheme.' In 1933, as a new year gift to its workers, and probably as a compensation for the privations, the firm increased the cover by 25 per cent while leaving the employee's contribution unchanged.

PENSION AND BENEFIT SCHEME
for Employees of
GEORGE BRETTLE & CO. LTD.

	Employees' Annual Earnings.	Amount of Annual Pension (payable monthly for life) from age 65.	Amount of Death Benefit.	Weekly Cost to Employee.
A.	£150 and under	£1 for each year of service	£100	1/-
B.	£151 to £250	£2 for each year of service	£200	2/-
C.	£251 to £400	£3 for each year of service	£300	3/-
D.	£401 to £500	£4 for each year of service	£400	4/-
E.	Over £500	£5 for each year of service	£500	5/-

Above: Brettles Pension Scheme leaflet (Photographer : Nick Lockett).

Meanwhile, Harry Twyford himself, whose main residence was in London, achieved social and civic prominence there. In 1929–30 he had acted as President of the appeal for the General Porters Benevolent Association, which had raised a record total.[14] In 1930 he was elected to the City's council, and a few months later, to the aldermanic bench as the representative for the ward of Cripplegate, and also served as a city magistrate. In 1934 he was elected Sheriff of the City, and in 1937 became Lord Mayor of London. To celebrate the occasion, all Belper employees of Brettles were invited to a dinner at the Drill Hall in Derby, and almost a thousand were present. Finally, in 1938 he was made a Knight of the British Empire (KBE), thus becoming 'Sir Harry'.

May 1929 General Election meeting at Oberon Pavilion. Speakers: Harry Twyford, Mr. Bowness & Mr. Wragg.

Above: Lord Mayor's Day 1888, the Procession passing the Mansion House depicted on 1937 Christmas card from Sir Harry & Lady Twyford.

Left: Sir Harry Twyford, Lord Mayor of London in his regalia.

THE MANSION HOUSE

DINNER

to the

London Staff of

George Brettle and Company Limited

on

Saturday, December 11th, 1937

by

The Right Hon. The Lord Mayor

Sir Harry Twyford

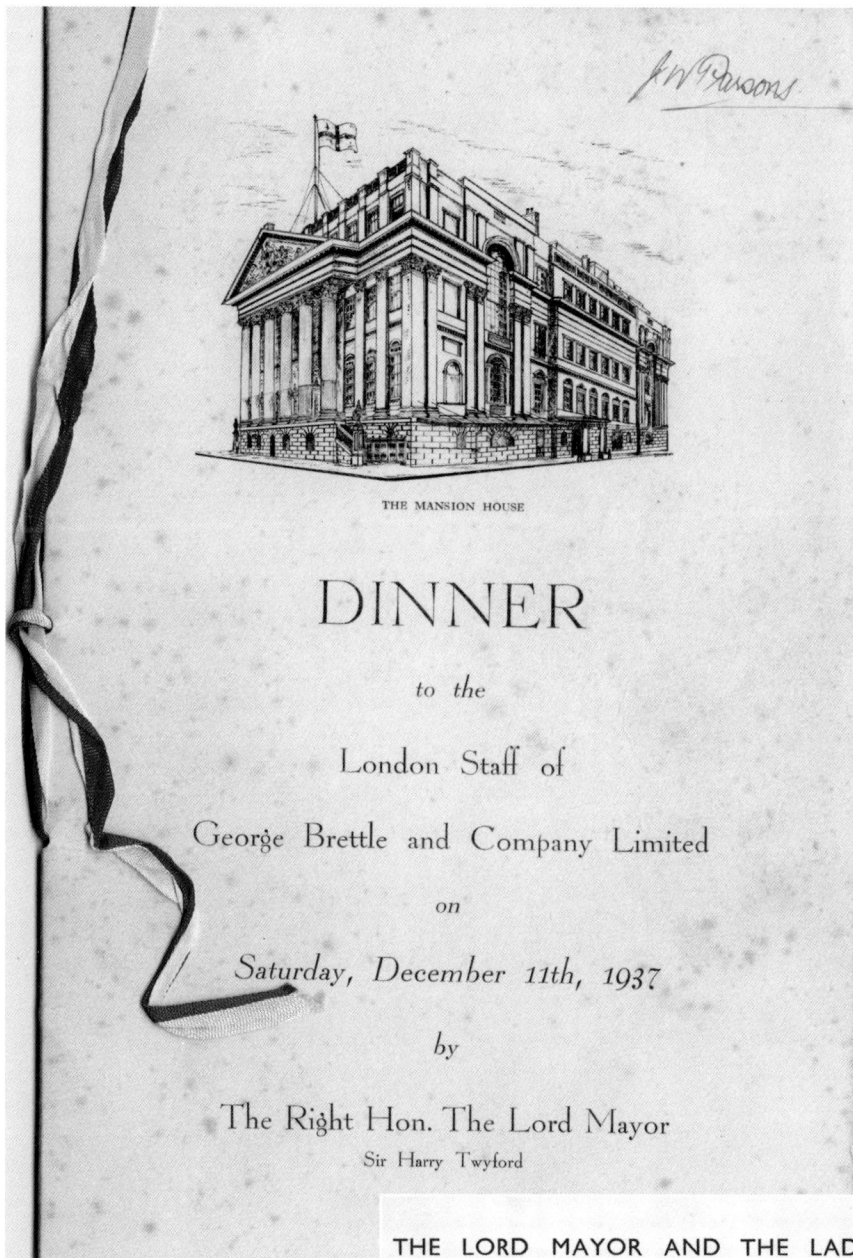

Above: Mansion House Dinner Menu, Programme & List of Guests, 11th December 1937.

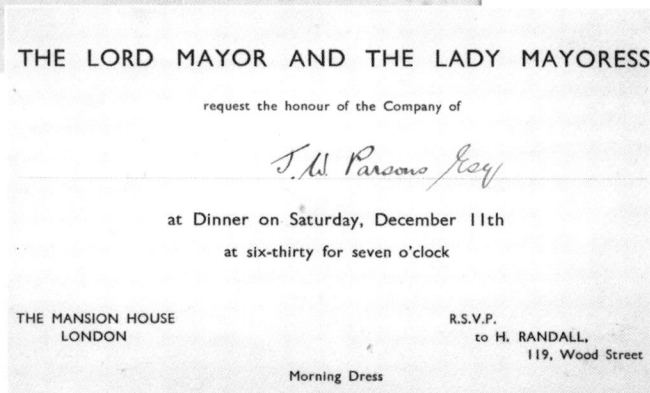

Right: Lord Mayor & Lady Mayoress Twyford dinner invitation to JW. Parsons.

THE LORD MAYOR AND THE LADY MAYORESS

request the honour of the Company of

J. W. Parsons Esq

at Dinner on Saturday, December 11th

at six-thirty for seven o'clock

THE MANSION HOUSE
LONDON

R.S.V.P.
to H. RANDALL,
119, Wood Street

Morning Dress

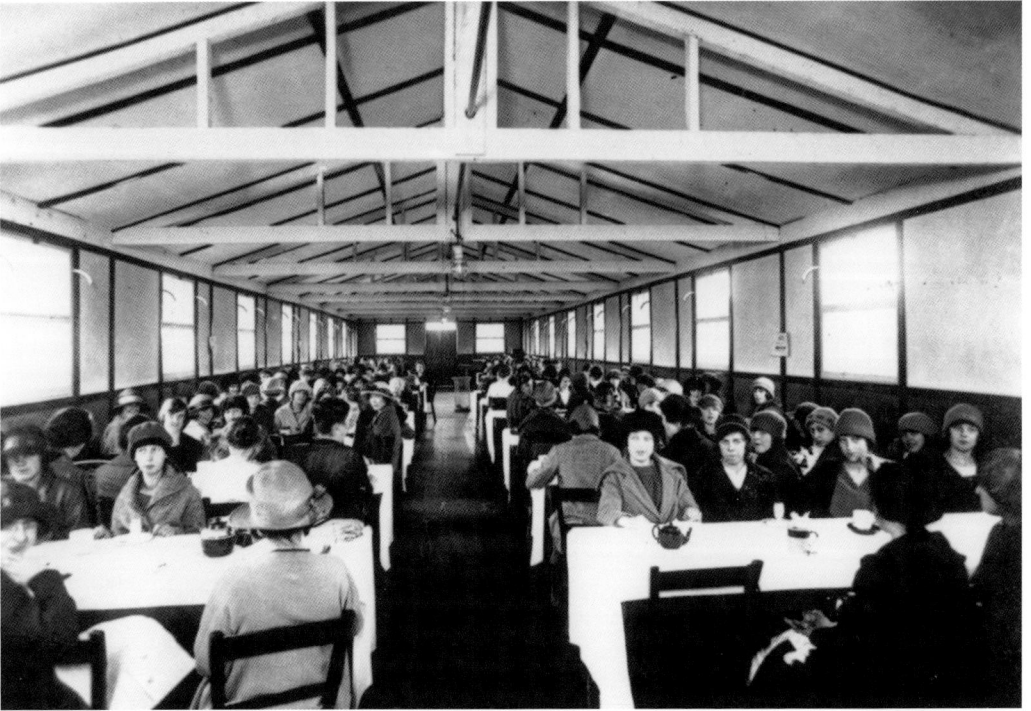

Canteen, Womens Room, June 1923.

Banquet given by Sir Harry Twyford, November 1937.

Sir Harry & Lady Twyford and Mr & Mrs Richard Twyford.

Sir Harry Twyford, Lord Mayor of London, Guildhall, 9th November 1937. Neville Chamberlain to the Mayors right hand.

Brettles Museum in Belper 1980s, showing the Browse Shield.

COLONIAL & FOREIGN AGENTS.

		Representing :—
Gollin & Co. Pty. Ltd.	17 Mincing Lane, E.C.	AUSTRALIA & NEW ZEALAND
,, ,, ,,	Pioneer House, York Street, Sydney	AUSTRALIA
,, ,, ,,	6 North Terrace, Adelaide	AUSTRALIA
,, ,, ,,	234/6 Flinders Lane, Melbourne	AUSTRALIA
,, ,, ,,	King Street, Perth	AUSTRALIA
,, ,, ,,	P.O. Box 913, 18 Victoria Street, Wellington	NEW ZEALAND
J. Y. Foster & Co.	P.O. Box 1436, Cape Times Building, 17 Church Street, Cape Town	SOUTH AFRICA
,, ,,	P.O. Box 5655, 9 President Buildings, Von Brandis Street, Johannesburg	
Edgar B. Walters Organisation	Bartholdi Building, 23rd Street and Broadway	NEW YORK.
S. E. Spence	242 St. James Street, Montreal	CANADA
Hilton & Inman	109 Wool Exchange, E.C.	INDIA
Michael Setton, Sons & Co.	P.O. Box 84, Cairo	EGYPT
,, ,, ,,	P.O. Box 519, Alexandria	
Joseph Dichy & Co.	P.O. Box 207, Beirut	SYRIA
Grigio Hermanos	Casilla 748, Buenos Aires	ARGENTINE
	Calle Mercedes 811, Montevideo	URUGUAY
Kolbjorn S. Hansen	Fredensborgveien 4, Oslo	NORWAY
A. Lucas	Vesterbrogade 5B, Copenhagen	DENMARK
Victor Hjorts	Brunkebergstorg 15, Stockholm	SWEDEN
Haardt & Lombardi	Via Spiga 22, Milan	ITALY
A. Lopez	Paz, 19 & 21, Madrid	SPAIN
W. H. Davis	39 Rue Lafayette, Paris	FRANCE
A. Nooteboom	19/21 Rosengracht, Amsterdam	HOLLAND
	13 Rue Madelaine, Brussels	BELGIUM
J. E. Pace ,, & Co.	225 Strada Sent' Ursola, Valletta	MALTA

Lisit of Colonial and Foreign Agents in 1914.

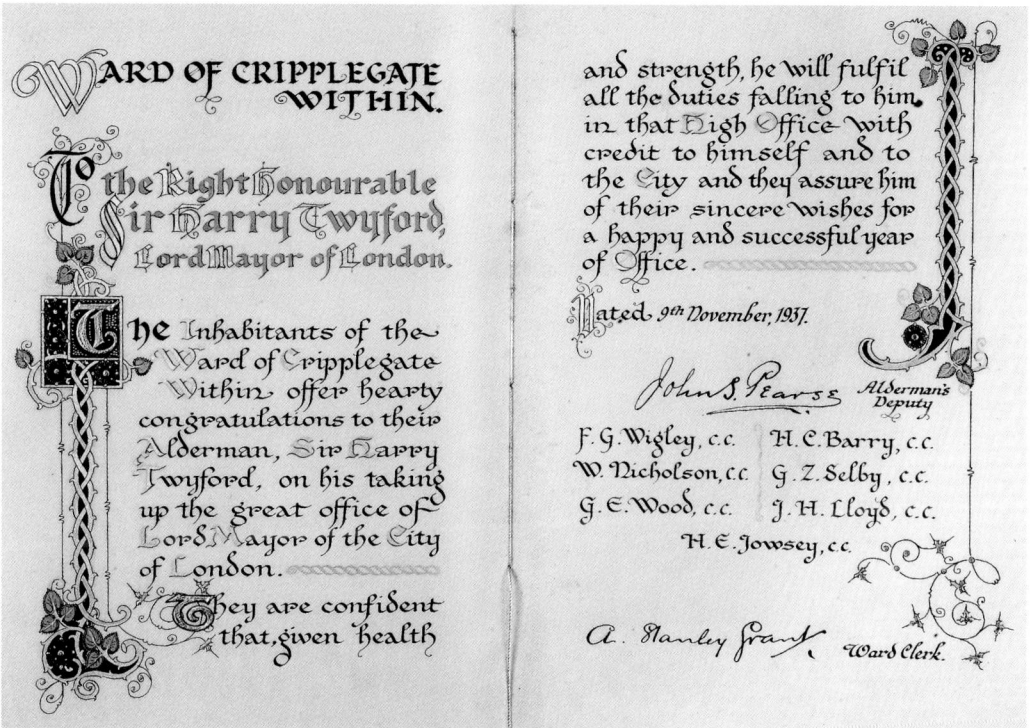

Cripplegate Complimentary letter to Harry Twyford, Lord Mayor of London, 1937 (Photographer: Nick Locket).

Left: Sir Harry Twyfords Medals (Photographer: Nick Locket).

Mansion House Visitors Book Signatures

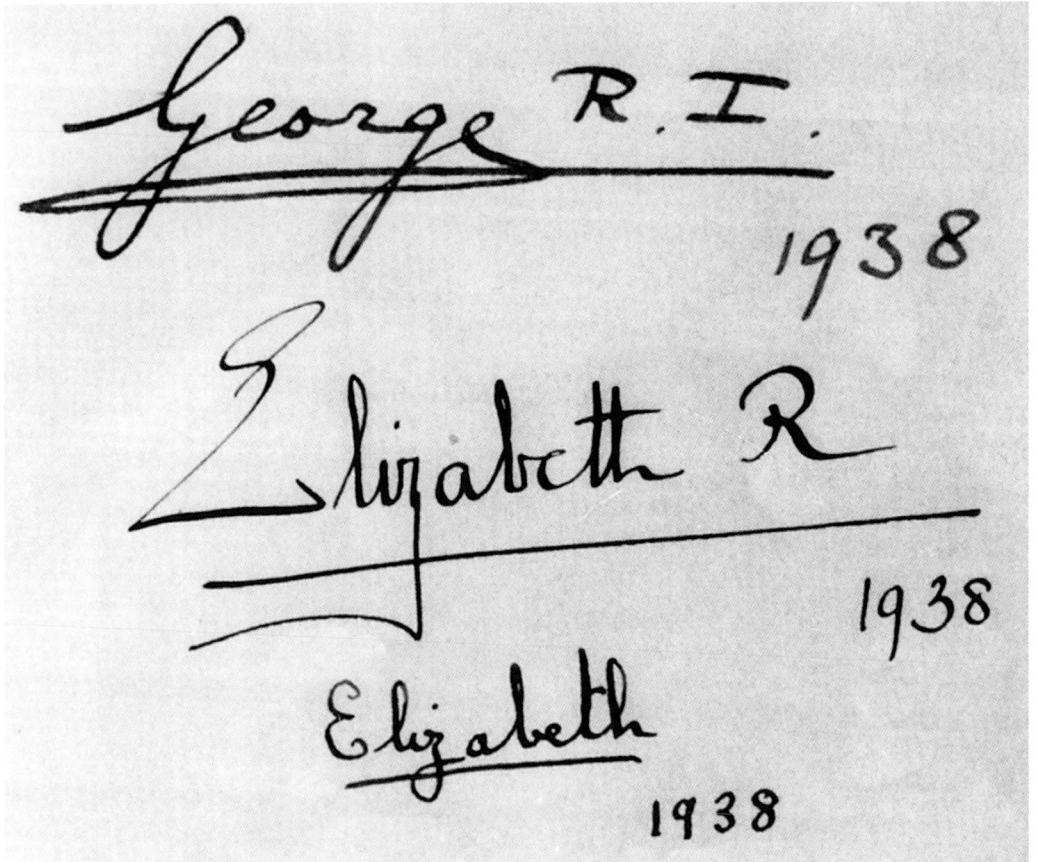

Signatures: King George & Queen Elizabeth 1938.

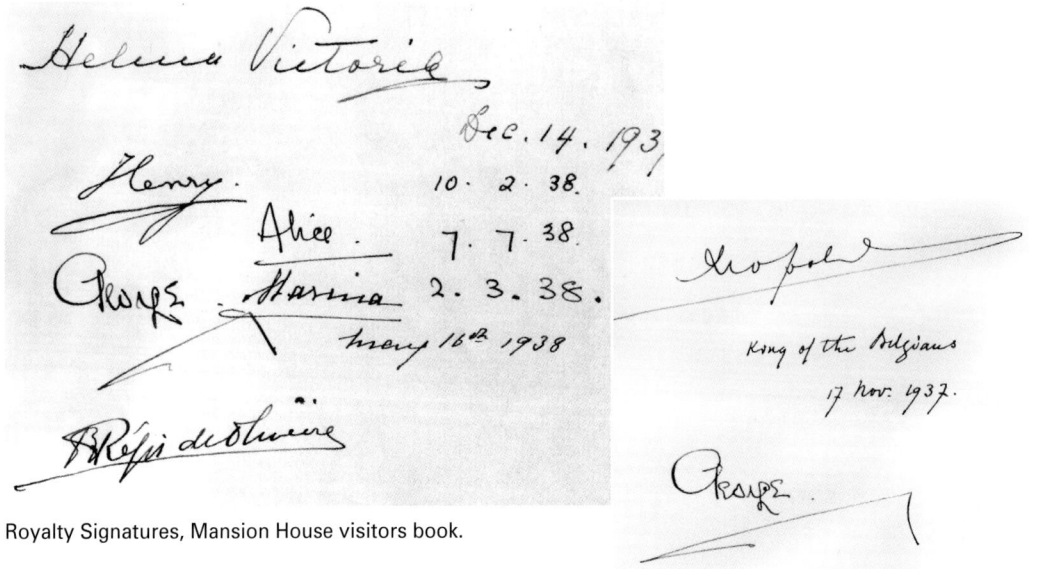

Royalty Signatures, Mansion House visitors book.

[Handwritten signatures in the Mansion House visitors book:]

Neville Chamberlain.

Cosmo Cantuar:

Hailsham
C

Stewart of Bury. C.J.

John Simon

[signature]

E de Cartier

Samuel Hoare:

[signature]

a. F. London:

[signature]

Government Signatures, Mansion House visitors book.

Going Public

In 1936, to raise more capital, Brettles changed from being a private to a partly public company. Its nominal capital was increased from £250,000 to £305,000, and the amount issued was increased from £202,000 to £301,874 by capitalising £99,274 of the undistributed profits. A new category of preference shares was created; these were sold at par to the British & Allied Investments Corporation and made available for dealing on the Stock Exchange. Thus, for the first time, a substantial amount of outside capital entered the firm. When the firm thus 'went public', the announcement in *The Times* described it as 'self-contained and believed to be equipped as one of the most up-to-date factories in the United Kingdom'.[15] The term 'self-contained' referred to the firm's machine-building activity, which continued until 1938. All in all, there was little resemblance between the firm on the eve of the First World War and that on the eve of the Second.

The Late 30s

Also around this time, there were several director changes. In 1933 F.J. Rayson retired as Director and Secretary after fifty-nine years of service, leaving Gibson and Dick Twyford the only directors for four years, under Sir Harry Twyford. Then, in 1937, Alfred Page was appointed to the Board. Page was a chartered accountant, for forty-seven years a member of Brettles' solicitors, Josolyne Miles, Page & Co. Since 1924 he had been special financial adviser to Brettles, a role which had clearly been appreciated. In 1938 Henry Osmont Randall was also made a Director. A native of Jersey, he had joined the firm as an apprentice in 1907, living above the Wood Street warehouse. He had worked in the Silk and Ladies Underwear departments, becoming Despatch Manager in 1926, and succeeding Rayson as Company Secretary in 1934.[16]

Of more impact on Belper, in 1937 the Factory Manager W.H. Bowness died; the entire factory was closed on the day of his funeral. He was succeeded by his deputy, John Ross, who had spent all his working life at Brettles. Starting at age 16 in 1900, he had become manager of the circular machine department during the First World War, then, in 1920, Deputy Manager of the factory under Bowness.

In the late 1930s there began to be a feeling that the styles of stockings being produced by the company were no longer up-to-date or smart enough. This case was made by Charles Doerr and Ivor Boyes, both then travellers for the Fancy Goods department, and much later to both become directors in the 1960s. As a consequence, it was decided to employ a designer named Alfred Weihs to develop the product lines, especially the fashionable varieties of knitted outerwear. Weihs was contracted to spend regular periods in Paris studying the latest fashions, as well as in Belper looking at the factory. But the designer was found to be 'very excitable and nervy', and after two valuable workers had resigned because of him it was decided to end his appointment. By then, the prospect of renewed European war had put paid to this development.

Second World War

The outbreak of war had a negative effect on the firm in various ways. First, with compulsory conscription, many male employees were called up into the armed forces, and most of their places had to be filled by women. A number of families faced financial difficulties with their menfolk away, and the firm paid allowances to them. Patriotic appeals led the company to invest in substantial quantities of government stock. Chairman Twyford visited the Belper factory in War Weapons Week and 'inspected the troops' in Belper Market Place. A more controversial incident was the sacking in 1940 of an employee who was a conscientious objector.

But the major effect of the war was the double bombing that destroyed the company's London premises of 130 years. Fortunately, the counting house and some other departments had been evacuated to Belper early in 1940. The first bomb fell on 119 Wood Street on the night of 10th November 1940, causing serious damage and destroying £61,891 worth of stock. The second fell on the night of 29th December, destroying the remaining £9,578 worth of stock and the building itself.

From a historian's point of view, the worst loss of the bombing was the destruction of virtually all the firm's financial records for the second half of the nineteenth century and the early years of the twentieth, making for an incomplete account of the firm's growth during those decades.

The famous Browse Shield (see Chapter 8) was saved from the ruins of Wood Street, and thence attained an even greater significance and reverence in Brettles minds, highly coveted and valued by those to whom this trophy was awarded from year to year. Today it resides in Belper North Mill Museum.

The firm took a temporary office in the Textile Exchange Buildings, and later in Regent Street. However, the whole commercial and warehouse side of the business was now moved to Belper at the beginning of 1941, as were all the employees except a skeleton office staff. This would have involved something of a squeeze physically, and five departments were closed down – Fancy Goods, 'Manchester Goods', Gloves, and Ladies and Gents Outfitting – departments that were heavily dependent on other suppliers rather than on what was produced at the Belper factory.

The war brought no boost to sales as the previous war had. Rather, following the Belper consolidation and closure of some departments, sales fell from just over £1.2m in 1940 to £753,164 in 1941, and reached their lowest point in 1942, at £620,293. The level of production fell too, due partly to the exodus of men and partly to the drop-off in demand. Both began to pick up in the last two years of the war, and were set to accelerate with the coming of peace.

Rather belatedly, in August 1944, the firm started a 'Contact' newsletter for its members serving in the forces, the first issue carrying a reassuring message by Harry Twyford, expressing appreciation for their brave efforts to 'maintain the empire' and the hope that their return home and to 'normal contact with the company' would not be long delayed. The newsletter listed two employee deaths, two missing, two wounded, one decorated 'DSM', one mentioned in despatches', and six prisoners-of-war – four in German hands and two in Japanese hands. The remaining pages were filled with letters from servicemen.

The second issue, issued in December 1944, listed four promotions, three of them to Major, and four discharged on medical grounds. Life was not put on hold for all – it also reported two marriages and one engagement. The 'Home News' section reported that the 'Comforts Fund' had benefitted over the previous two years from the proceeds of two 'Oberon Concert Parties' arranged by Mr E.H. Meredith; also that the Cricket XI had kept going, with the empty places being filled by employees in their fifties who had escaped call-up. Despite this they had done well, playing 18 matches, of which they had won eight, drawn six and lost only four (more on this in Chapter 8).[17]

Number 3 must have been an interesting newsletter, coming out in 1945 around the time of victory, but unfortunately it has not survived. It was of course some time after this before most of the troops were discharged, and the last issue, number 4, came out in February 1946. It reported three army promotions, two marriages, three births, and one death in Japanese hands on 28th October 1944. By mid 1946 most of the serving employees had returned, and the 'Contact' newsletter was discontinued.

North view of Factory in snow, 27th January 1940.

Sir Harry Twyford inspecting troops, War Weapons Week, March 1941.

War Weapons Week, Belper Market Place, March 1941.

Brettles Christmas Party, 1940s.

6. THE POST-WAR PERIOD

There had been a few management changes during the early 1940s. In 1941 Alfred Page had died and A.M. Gibson had retired from directorship, whereupon Ernest Edward Hall had been made a director. Hall had been employed by the firm since he joined as an apprentice in 1896, had been trained by John Scott and in 1914 had become buyer for the Lisle department. He had then sat on the board for five years alongside H.O. Randall and Harry Twyford before retiring in 1946.

Thereupon Hall's seat as director was offered to W.H. Inch, another long-serving employee. Inch had joined in 1908 as an apprentice at Wood Street, transferred to the counting house in 1910, becoming its manager in 1933, and had moved to Belper with the others in 1941.

Following the destruction of 119 Wood Street by bombing, the London activities had been relocated to Belper in 1941, but a complete separation was maintained between this and the manufacturing side (the factory). The wholesale side, including the warehouse, was still referred to as the 'London side'. Staff were very aware of an elitism shown by and accorded to the latter, such that even staff in the 'Counting House' which served the 'London side' felt superior to those in the Wages office which served the factory! This demarcation persisted for over twenty years.

Trade was beginning to pick up as the war ended. The number of commercial visitors to the firm rose from 444 in 1944 and 665 in 1945 to 765 in 1946 and nearly a thousand in 1947. Sales that year were over £930,000, and in 1948 reached the pre-war level of £1.2 million. The rate of profit, which had remained between 7 and 8 per cent from 1940 to 46, reached 9 per cent in 1947 and 11 per cent in 1948.

There were, however, problems on the supply side – continuing shortages of yarn and of fuel, and the virtual impossibility of obtaining new machinery to gradually replace the ageing equipment. Both British and American machines were in very short supply, and it became advantageous for firms to 'club together' in their purchase and use of new machines.[1] Brettles' response this time was not to build their own machines as they had done before the war; the sort needed in the late 1940s were much bigger and more sophisticated. Rather, in 1946 they began a rather strange association with a much smaller firm, the Charnos Hosiery Company, owned by Charles Noskwith. In exchange for a deal on machine purchases, Brettles provided two loans to Charnos for new factory premises at Ilkeston, east of Belper, and agreed to buy a large proportion of their output.

In 1947 two of the very latest fine-gauge 30-at-once hosiery machines made in Pennsylvania were obtained for £10,000 each. They were ordered by Charnos but then purchased from that firm by Brettles, who from then on continued to replace and add to their stock of machinery. Output then grew some more, and by 1949 it exceeded the production level in the boom years of the 1920s, and continued to increase to three-quarters of a million pounds in 1951, whilst actual sales reached two million pounds. Where was it all going? Certainly, exports were growing, and there were now sales agents in 14 countries – in Australia, New Zealand, Egypt, India, Burma, South Africa and Canada, as well as in France, Belgium, Holland, Denmark, Norway, Sweden and Italy.

Another major problem in the late 1940s was the shortage of labour. Even at the end of 1946, it was proving difficult to get sufficient linkers and seamers to process the work of the knitters. In 1948 management investigated some premises near Chesterfield as a possible place to tap a new source of female labour, and later that year they even considered looking to Tyneside for 'finishing labour'. In 1949 a large house was purchased as a hostel for 20 to 30 'German refugee girls'.

A 1947 essay on Belper (author unknown, but held at St John's Chapel) states:

> The principal industry at Belper is not cotton but hosiery, there being many firms in the town producing a multiplicity of goods, including underwear and outerwear. Of these, the most important is Messrs George Brettle & Co. Ltd . . . It now stands in its own grounds of 23 acres, of which 7.5 acres are built on, and employs some eight hundred workers. The raw materials from which they manufacture are silk, previously from Macclesfield [now from Strutts?], cotton from Lancashire, wool from Yorkshire, rayon from Coventry, Birmingham, Liverpool and Aintree, and nylon from Courtaulds at Coventry.

Relationship Problems

In the late 1940s some personality clashes arose between managers. In 1946, Dick Twyford had returned from military service as a major. He was made Director in charge of the production side and instructed to work closely with John Ross, the Factory Manager, without interfering with the latter's duties. That proved to be difficult! In November 1946, on the eve of a trip overseas, Sir Harry made an appeal for 'unity and friendly relations' while he was away, which was recorded in the Directors' minute book. But the minutes record that, after management discussions, some decisions could not be agreed and were deferred until Harry's return.

Factory unity under Dick Twyford proved impossible, and within a year John Ross took early retirement. He was succeeded as Factory Manager by Walter Bennett, a newcomer to the firm, who had been the Technical Manager for R. Rowley & Co. Ltd, hosiery manufacturers at Leicester, and a lecturer at Loughborough Technical College. Bennett held the gold medal of the Worshipful Company of Framework Knitters and the silver medal of the City and Guilds of the London Institute. Harte comments that a good deal of the factory's subsequent success in the 1950s was due to Bennett's technical and managerial abilities, just as it had been to those of Bowness in the 1920s.[2]

Ross's retirement did not bring unity, however. Dick Twyford was still a factor, and some kind of unpleasantness arose between Bennett and E.H. Meredith, the Sock department buyer. Sir Harry attempted to restore peace by offering both of them seats on the board. He was, however, deeply displeased by whatever had happened, and stated that if anything similar were to happen again 'he would place his shares on the market and the company would lose its present private control'.

But Sir Harry also had reasons of his own for wishing to do so. In January 1948, In view of his advancing age and the prospect of heavy death duties, he changed the company's articles and the firm became a fully public company, with the sale of 300,000 ordinary shares with a nominal value of five shillings each. By the end of the year there were over two thousand shareholders. In 1950 more finance was raised when the share capital was increased to £405,000 by the creation of 400,000 new shares. A final capitalisation of £100,750 was made in 1954.

In May 1951 Sir Harry announced that he was pleased by the better feelings among the directors, and asked them to approve Dick Twyford's appointment as Deputy Chairman, which they duly did.

Womens Wear News of that year included a Brettles page in its 'Personality Parade' series, with a large photograph of 'Major H.R. Twyford, Deputy Chairman and Joint Managing Director' alongside that of 'Sir Harry Twyford KBE, Chairman and Joint Managing Director' and smaller pictures of five other directors. It states:

> The business was converted into a private family company in 1914 and a Public Company in 1936. Most of the Directors have spent practically all their business lives in the service of the Company – Mr. H.O. Randall (Secretary) since 1907, Mr. W.H. Inch (Counting House Manager) from 1908, Mr. E.H. Meredith (Buyer) since 1911, Sir Harry Twyford 1913 and Major H.R. Twyford 1919.[3]

But three years later there was another personality crisis involving Dick Twyford, and this time he resigned. In March 1954 he was given leave of absence until he reached the age of 55 in the September, when the firm was able to give him a pension.

The Shop Floor

By now the company had a large factory workforce, each of whom were provided with a Brettles 'Employees Handbook'. This interesting booklet describes the business carried on by the company as 'the manufacture of ladies' and girls' fashioned stockings, children's socks and underwear for men, women and children'. It claims that 'since the end of the war, considerable extension and replacement of plant and machinery as well as modernisation of buildings has been carried out at considerable cost, so that all machinery is up-to-date, and the working conditions throughout the business brought as near to perfection as possible'.

So what were these working conditions? It states that 'the normal working hours for factory operatives and staff' were 8am to 5.55pm, whilst 'office and clerical staff' started at 8.30am and finished at 5pm. All staff shared the same lunch hour of 12.25 to 1.25pm and it would appear that this was unpaid, though they were allowed a ten-minute paid break mid morning and mid afternoon. These hours of work were said to be 'determined by and based upon the joint agreement between the National Union of Hosiery Workers and the National Hosiery Manufacturers Federation'.

The booklet is less specific about pay, but states that 'most of the processes in the Factory and Dyeworks are on a piece-rate basis' and that 'these rates are regulated by the National Joint Industrial Council'. One employee issued with the handbook was N. Chamberlain, who wrote on the first page that he had started work in 1928 at just eight shillings a week, back in those non-union days. What progress they must have seen.

The booklet describes the 'Ticketograph' system then 'in operation for all processes up to dyeing and finishing of hose and children's socks, and for underwear from the cutting stage onwards . . . A ticketograph ticket is made out for each ten dozen lot of children's socks, each five dozen lot of ladies' hose and one dozen of underwear'. Employees were responsible for ensuring that every 'lot' had a ticket when the work was given out to them and when it was returned as completed. This then fed into the make-up of wages which were 'computed by the Factory Counting House Staff'.[4]

Above: Factory front, 1950s and **below** Factory North Corner, 1950s.

The Counting House

In September of 1951, Syd Clarke, one of the sources for this book, who had been in the RAF, joined the company and was employed in the Belper Counting House with a Mr Ernest Staings who had worked there for most of his life, both of them working under W.H. Inch.

Syd spent much of his time between Mondays and Thursdays working out the wages for the factory production and office staff, helped by eight female staff, and all worked out manually. On Fridays, Ernest and Syd went by taxi to the National Provincial (later Nat West) Bank – always at the same time! – to pick up the cash, then returned to 'bag' it for each department and make up the individual envelopes, and everything had to be balanced to the exact old penny. Then each member of the Counting House had a department to pay out. Syd recalls that there were ten departments to pay: Hosiery Knitters (men), Seaming Room (ladies), Footers and Heelers (ladies), Menders ('rough' and 'finished'), Hosiery Finishing, Socks department (knitted and finished), Underwear, Dye House (dying and preboarding), Circular or Web Knitting (men) and Office Weekly. The few monthly salaries were paid into bank accounts at the end of the month. Syd also helped Ernest Staings with the Purchase Ledger (mainly of yarn for knitting, from British Nylon Spinners), the Petty Cash and Cash Book and the Nominal Ledger of Assets, and they produced a complete year-end Profit and Loss Account.

By the early 50s there was again a small London showroom at 48 Conduit Street in Mayfair, next to the Westbury Hotel. Confusingly, the wholesale activities at Belper were still referred to as 'the London side', and Syd Clarke recalls that:

> Goods knitted for the London side were invoiced out to the warehouse and credited in the Belper or Factory side, which had to be balanced monthly, and a cheque was actually sent from the London side to the Counting House and paid into the bank! The two were treated as separate companies all year, until the year end when they were 'amalgamated' in the accounts.[5]

Another of Syd's memories from the early 1950s was the monthly sales of 15 & 30 denier nylon stockings held in the former Wards building, at 7/6d a pair. For most people, these had been almost impossible to obtain during the war years, and now they were in great demand, with queues stretching round the car park.

Director Changes in the 1950s

Following Dick Twyford's retirement, two new directors were appointed at the beginning of 1955, neither of them full-time and both brought in from outside the firm. F.M. Welsford had been a solicitor at the Biddle, Thorne, Welsford & Barnes partnership, and R.B. Wynne had been the company's bank manager at the National Provincial Bank! Wynne became Deputy Chairman after Dick Twyford's departure and later became Managing Director after Sir Harry's resignation of that post in 1960.

There were several director retirements in these years, starting with E.H. Meredith in 1954. Then W.H. Inch and H.O. Randall, the Company Secretary, both with over fifty years' service, retired at the same time in January 1959. W.H. Inch was succeeded as Counting House Manager by C. Haskell, who had joined the firm's Counting House in 1926 and been appointed Chief Cashier in 1951.

But H.O. Randall's responsibilities were split. He was succeeded as Company Secretary by Mr. P.A. Nash, who had joined the Counting House in 1928 and been Assistant Credit Manager since 1951. Meanwhile C.G. Gosling was appointed to succeed him as Warehouse Manager and Staff Manager. He had joined the firm in 1925 and been a traveller in Kent and in North and East London, and had been appointed Sales Manager in 1949. Gosling's position as Sales Manager was taken by Charles J. Doerr, who had joined the firm in 1927 and served in the Entering Room and then the Lisle department until 1946, before becoming a traveller in South Yorkshire and Lincolnshire.[6] Later, in 1961, a third part-time director was brought in – W.B. Ross Collins, a partner in the insurance brokers Sedgewick Collins & Co.

During the 1950s, the shareholders were well looked after in terms of dividends. Between 1948 and 1949, annual dividends of 7.5 per cent had been paid. Following increased profitability, this rose to 12.5 per cent in 1950, to 15 per cent in 1953 and to a peak of 20 per cent in 1956. Thereafter, profits began to fall, and dividends returned to 15 per cent in 1957, then to 10 per cent in the following two years.[7]

Circular or Rotary Knitting Machines.

Circular or Rotary Knitting Machines.

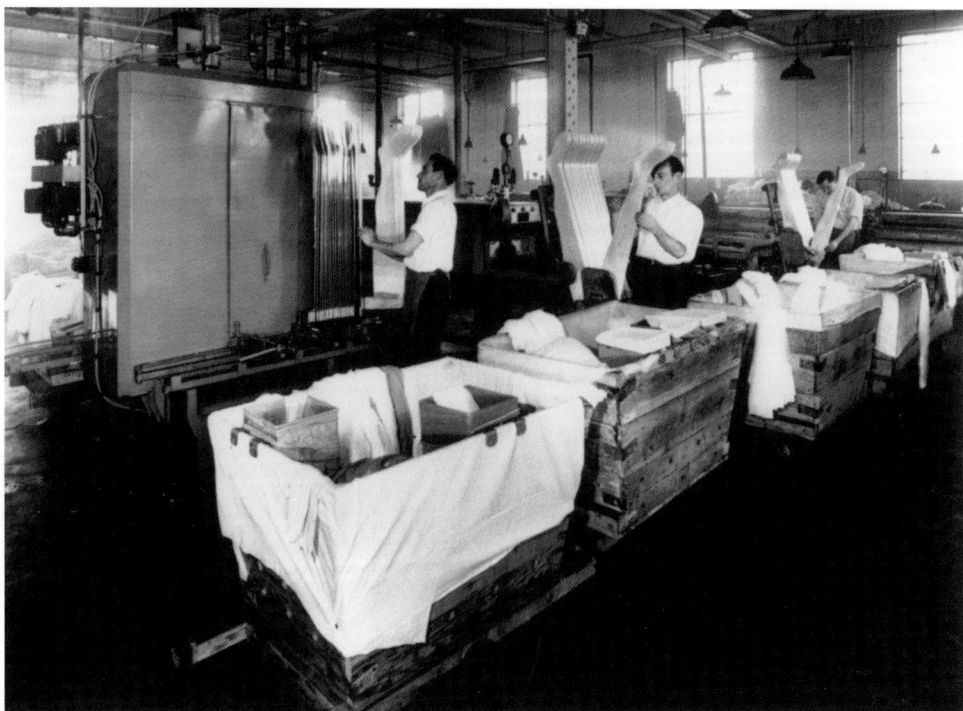

Pre-Boarding of Stockings, 1950s.

Arthur Smith, Fully fashioned Knitting, 1950s.

Brettles men at Summer School (1952 – 1957)

Bill Aldread being welcomed to Worcester college Oxford 1952.

1952 Summer School (Sandy Taylor on left, Bill Aldred on right).

1953, Worcestor College, Oxford (From Left: T. Brown, P. Nash, S. Gibson, G. Poole).

1957, Worcester College, Oxford (Left to Right: D. Wingfield, T. Brown, J. Parker).

Reprinted from the "Derbyshire Advertiser," January 16th, 1959

BELPER DIRECTORS RETIRE

Two directors of George Brettle and Co. Ltd , Belper, whose total service with the firm is over a hundred years, are to retire from active service on Monday.

They are Mr. H. O. Randall, a director, secretary and warehouse manager, of 295, Duffield-road, Allestree; and Mr. W. H. Inch, director and counting house manager, of 395, Duffield-road, Allestree.

Both Mr. Randall and Mr. Inch started with the firm as apprentices, when it had premises in London. Like all the other apprentices of their day, they lived above the firm's warehouse.

Mr. Randall joined the firm in 1907. A native of Jersey, he served in the silk and ladies' underwear departments. In 1926, he was appointed dispatch manager, in 1933 he became secretary and in 1938 was made a director.

He served with the R.A.M.C. and London Rifle Brigade in the 1914-18 war in Egypt and Palestine.

Mr. Inch joined the firm in 1908 and two years later went into the counting house. He became manager of the counting house in 1933 and in 1946 was made a director.

A native of Wisbech, Mr. Inch served with the Kensington Battalion (London Regiment) and in the Machine Gun Corps during the 1914-18 war. He saw active service in France where he was wounded. Later he became a Second Lieutenant in the K.R.R.

The London premises of Messrs. Brettle was destroyed during the 1939-45 war and the staff were moved to Belper.

Mr. C. G. Gossling, who was appointed director last year, is to succeed Mr. Randall as warehouse manager and staff manager.

Mr. Gossling joined the firm in 1925 and was a traveller in the Kent district and in East and North London. He was appointed sales manager in 1949.

Mr. C. Haskell has been appointed Counting House Manager to succeed Mr. Inch. Mr. Haskell joined the firm in 1926 and in 1951 was appointed chief cashier.

Mr. C. J. Doerr will take over as sales manager from Mr. Gossling. After joining the firm in 1927, he served in various departments and then became a traveller in South Yorks and Lincolnshire.

Mr. P. A. Nash, who joined the firm in 1928, has been appointed secretary. In 1951 he was made assistant credit manager.

Belper Directors Retire, January 1959 (Standing: C. Haskell, C.J. Doerr, P.A. Nash. Sitting: W.H. Inch, H.O. Randall, C.G. Gosling).

Life on the Shop Floor

The ordinary workers were mostly unconcerned with such things, and the camaraderie of daily life in the factory continued the same. It is well described by a poem from this period called 'Flimsy Girl':

> Nowt but a slip of a thing, swapped school for Brettles.
> 'You'll be on the flimsies' they said, and in my head
> Were wings, a sort of ballet flapping perhaps – but instead
> I was left in a room with a sheaf of thin paper, alone.
>
> I went bonkers, so I left there for the dyeworks
> And onto the half hose. We sat, long poles between our legs
> To turn the socks, then stack according to their tags.
> The girls were alright, but after a day, did my knees ache.
>
> Young we were, and scornful of the older ones' 'tut, tut, tut'.
> We'd just chatter, turn up the latest hits on the radio.
> 'Oh Carol' it sang, don't think of your work tomorrow,
> Get home, doll up for a night of jiving at the Regal or Troc.
>
> Morning after town, there'd be a roar and 'Jump on' from this lad,
> So I did, 'cause if you were late, they'd dock your money off.
> Then at work, we'd chew the fat, us girls, and have a laugh,
> But then go quiet; we wouldn't want to see our Mr Winkler cross.
>
> Between my childhood and settling down as wife and mother
> Were those sticky nights of teddy boys and brothel creepers,
> High heel shoes, the dancing frocks, that 'Oh Carol' from the speakers,
> The piecework days of turning socks, packing, checking jumpers.[8]

Exit Strategy

Slowly, Sir Harry began to shed his responsibilities. In 1960, at the age of 90, he gave up being Managing Director but continued as Chairman. There were management concerns about the succession. After all, four times previously owners of the firm had died without a natural successor within the firm – in 1835, 1871, 1882 and 1913 – and the first three of these occasions were each accompanied by an upheaval in the firm's affairs. (On the fourth, Harry Twyford had taken over.)

It must have been a disappointment to the grand old man that his hopes for Dick Twyford to succeed him had come to nothing, and from this point it appears that he tried to sell the company. In 1961 there were negotiations with a possible buyer of the firm's issued ordinary shares. The offer was ten shillings per share, which totalled a little over £600,000 when the firm's net assets were valued in its own books at over £824,000. Sir Harry refused to sell for less than eleven shillings per share, and the offer was rejected – a mistake, in retrospect.

The lowest profits came in 1963; a small 5 per cent dividend was still paid, but financed out of reserves.[9] In March 1963, at the age of 93, Sir Harry resigned as Chairman but remained a member of the Board, and R.B. Wynne became the new Chairman. Taking account of recent poor performance, another buyer offered 7/6d per share. Harry now seemed resigned to selling at a low price, and advised the directors accordingly, but they rejected the offer in November.

In early December Wynne suggested an offer be invited from Courtaulds, which duly happened. Courtaulds offered one of their ordinary £1 stock units for ten of Brettles' ordinary shares, and five of their 6 per cent preference shares for six of Brettles' 5 per cent preference shares. The total value of the offer was £465,000, when Brettles was valued in its own books at £780,000. By Christmas it was decided to accept their terms. Courtaulds had got a bargain, and the new year would bring a new era.

Sold to Courtaulds

The first few weeks of 1964 saw Brettles beginning to undergo changes comparable to those which took place after 1913 under Harry Twyford. By the end of January, Twyford, Welsford and Collins had retired as directors – Sir Harry after serving for fifty years. He retired to Sidmouth, and ensured the respected memory he left behind in Belper by leaving £200 to each of some 200 pensioners of the firm. After just over three years of retirement, he died at Sidmouth in 1967.

In early 1964 three Courtaulds men were appointed to take the places of those who had retired: T.P. Jennison, G.H. Tarrant and C.W. Powell. Wynne retired as Managing Director in May and as Chairman in September, and was replaced in these capacities by Powell and Jennison respectively. There were, however, still some directorships from old Brettles men: J.L. Bush (Merchandise) and C.G. Gosling (Administration) continued, Charles Doerr (Sales) was appointed, and later Ivor Boyes. Doerr and Boyes had both started their careers as travellers for the Fancy Goods department, and became directors under Courtaulds management.

7. THE COURTAULDS YEARS

Thus 1964 was the first year of Brettles under Courtaulds, no doubt an uncertain time for managers and staff alike. For the short term, T.P. Jennison and George Tarrant were appointed as Directors early in the year, and R.B. Wynne retired as Managing Director in May and as Chairman in September. Courtaulds established Brettles' new management team of Charles Powell as Managing Director, J.L. Bush as Merchandise Director, Jack Price as Financial Director and C.J. Doerr as Sales Director. Powell, a long-term Courtaulds executive who had been based at their Coventry headquarters, came to combine the offices of Chairman and Managing Director as Wynne had done earlier. As MD he reported to the Courtaulds Hosiery divisional director, who in turn reported to the main management board, within which Lord Kearton and Sir Christopher Hogg held the top jobs.

The immediate experience of staff was a tightening up of discipline. For example, up to this time, at 11am and again at 4pm every day, in their 'quarter-hour coffee break', some of the Buyers left the main building and headed over the road to the Lion Hotel. This was of course outside normal licensing hours, but clearly the hotel bar was an attraction, and beyond this we can only speculate! After the takeover, however, these trips to the Lion were promptly stopped.

The acquisition of Brettles was just a beginning. It was soon decided that Brettles should become the main hosiery production unit of the Courtaulds group. Courtaulds apparently intended to control the hosiery market, for in 1965 it acquired four other similar though smaller companies – Hartwood Hosiery (who supplied Littlewoods and Woolworths), F.W. Sellers (who supplied Boots and Woolworths), Tor Hosiery of Matlock, and Play Girl Nylons, which all became part of Brettles.

All this required changes. First, non-hosiery activities had to be shed to other companies within the group. Syd Clarke of the Counting House recalls:

> They took over and they only wanted the Knitted and Dyehouse departments, so I was joined up with the Company Accountant on the London side (warehouse) to help join the two together, helped by the incoming financial people of Courtaulds, mainly from Spondon (East Derby). Mr. J.A. Price was my new boss. Others in my office from Belper after 1964 were accountants Bob Foster (transferred from Spondon) and Peter Curl, who was new.

Secondly, there had to be a reorganisation of production. During the previous hundred years, small extra buildings and extensions had been continually added with little thought to overall planning. This resulted in an elegant but sprawling collection of buildings with a range of disconnected activities being undertaken. Therefore a work study graph of the time traced the movement of goods during production as a zig-zag line, which told its own story of to-and-fro backtracking. The challenge now was to replace this with a continuous semi-circular line representing a logical and efficient flow of production from yarn store to despatch. This was no mean task and required radical changes.

In March 1966 Oswald Hibbert moved from Blount and Co., another Courtaulds subsidiary, to succeed Walter Bennett as the Production Director. In a press statement he stated: 'Mass production is the only way to compete today. We are utilising every square inch of space, and the key to the whole thing is a vastly improved work flow. We have plans to go still further, and all improvements are being made with further expansion in mind.'[1]

By 1967 the Belper factory was only producing knitted stockings and tights, whilst other production had been moved to factories elsewhere. The sock and half-frame machines were moved to the factory of Messrs Meridian at Ilkeston. The machinery of the Underwear Knitting section was moved, some to Meridian at Nottingham and some to Foster, Clay & Ward at Middlesbrough – both Courtaulds subsidiaries. This cleared the decks for the much-needed improvement of workflow in stocking production at Belper. All single-feed machines were scrapped, and the new plant included 120 eight-feed Zodiacs, various twin-feed equipment, Marshall Arm conveyors and two Bentley reciprocated-heel machines. By these means, stocking production was increased by 150 per cent.

These changes were said to be brought about without any redundancies amongst the company's staff of 881. Management engendered a productivity-conscious climate, and sought to involve staff in the vision in various ways, including a monthly £10 prize and smaller prizes for ideas that would boost efficiency. Production meetings of all managers were held every two weeks. The main customer was now Marks and Spencer.

Manufacturing and Sales Divided

In 1967, the Brettles company was split into two divisions of Courtaulds. The factory side, whilst remaining George Brettle & Co. Ltd. for the time being, came under Courtaulds' Hosiery division along with Hartwood Hosiery, F.W. Sellers, Blount & Co. and Aristoc, whilst the warehouse and shop came under Courtaulds' Distributors division along with Cooke Watts, Tagge, Holts of Leeds and Samuel Farmer of Leicester, and took the name of 'Brettles Sales'. Whilst Brettles had narrowed its production range since the early 60s, however, Brettles Sales was able to diversify its product range.

By the early 1970s, the two halves had become new Courtaulds companies. George Brettle & Co. Ltd. had become Courtaulds Hosiery Ltd, with David Fry as Managing Director, one of the Fry family of chocolate fame. Meanwhile the wholesale side had become Courtaulds Distributors Ltd, trading as Brettles Sales, with Mr C. Gosling as Managing Director, thus indicating that the old name 'Brettles' was to be preserved only as a well-known trading name.

From this point, our story is mainly that of Brettles Sales. At first, Mr J.L. Bush was as Merchandise Director, then Ivor Boyes. In 1972 Boyes became Managing Director, and Tony Gray took his place as Merchandise Director. Tony had worked for Kayser Bondor, a major lingerie producer, and had joined Brettles in 1964 as a lingerie buyer, but had found the product range somewhat dated; for example it included 40 styles of pyjamas and a large selection of nightdresses, including winceyette, all long length! Tony had updated the range, and added housecoats, which was a great success and doubled turnover. In making these changes, Tony recalls that he forged a good working relationship with David Fry, the MD of Courtaulds Hosiery, whose interests included cricket and jazz.

Tony started a regular sales conference which brought together buyers and sales staff and at which new ranges were introduced. These were held first at Nottingham University, and later at the New Bath Hotel (Matlock Bath), the Peveril of the Peak Hotel (Dovedale), the Makeney Hall Hotel (Derby), Ashbourne Gateway Hotel, and further afield at Hinckley Island and Stratford-upon-Avon. Working with the Scotland sales representative, Tony led a first-ever sales and marketing drive to the Shetland and Orkney Isles which was very successful. Tony also remembers organising and going on trade missions to Nigeria (which brought £50k worth of sales), New Zealand, Japan, and one to Panama that was sponsored by the British Overseas Trade Board.

Internal Organisation

The names of the departments at this time show the widening of the product range. Each was headed by its own Buyer, also known as Merchandiser, for example George Wyatt for the Ladies Underwear & Woven department. Of seven Buyers known to have operated during the early 1970s, at least five had been commercial travellers for the company – Leo Collins (Children's Clothing), Doug Penton (Lingerie), Sandy Taylor (Casuals), Michael Hayman (Hosiery) and Graham Newton (Menswear). This perhaps indicates the promotion opportunities that existed and that the company rewarded experience and merit.

Beneath the Buyer of each department was a Supervisor or 'first man', then typists, porters, 'enterers' (who manually wrote out dockets) and 'order pullers' – such quaint terms remained.

The Despatch department (including the 'entering room') was managed by Denis Campbell and employed at least 16 workers. Here, goods from each department were assembled and matched to the delivery dockets, then packed and despatched. During the busy seasons of spring and autumn, the Despatch department often became inundated with boxed merchandise, chutes became overloaded, and 'wheelers' lined up waiting in train-like fashion.

Another key department was Accounts (still known as the 'Counting House'), within which Syd Clarke was the Accountant, Peter Knight the Credit Controller and Paul Naylor the Assistant. A fuller account of the departments follows in Chapter 9.

The Lighter Side

Work life was not all serious. Former employees remember that occasionally, when pressure of work was not so great, you could pull a 'wheeler' out from under a bench and find some worker in there, either sleeping or put there for a joke if they were a new starter. The chutes that came from the departments on the higher floors were not only used to send goods down to Despatch, but sometimes a new recruit or trainee would be sent down the chute, on the pretext that this was normal! Other well-known pranks were to send newcomers to get 'fixture stretchers' (fixtures were shelves) or 'long weights', or to tell them to send water-softening tablets out with the swimwear!

There were no longer separate men's and women's canteens as in the early years, but there were separate staff and management canteens. The canteen was used for a variety of social events, including dances and discos. It would seem that the company also catered for the spiritual needs of its workers, and Syd Clarke remembers that the Methodist minister acted as a chaplain and visited a different department each day, and used to say grace at the annual staff Christmas dinner.

The festive season was celebrated well. Christmas lunches were held in the canteen, and were served to the staff by management. Michael Hayman and Leo Collins were well known for serving in fancy dress. Festivities often continued in the local pubs. Also, many employees invited their colleagues to their birthday and other parties; the pubs and clubs of Derby were popular venues. This writer was passed two wedding photographs of the period, both consisting mainly of Brettles staff, no doubt colleagues of the bride or groom (or both). The company also supported its own football, cricket, table tennis, darts, dominoes and other sports teams, which mostly still bore the historic Oberon name (see Chapter 8).

New Staff and Director Changes

On 30th July 1973 something happened that probably seemed quite unimportant at the time. Gary Spendlove started work at Brettles, in the Despatch office, which had up to forty staff. None could have guessed then that this young man would one day be the means of the Brettles brand's survival. Gary became a trainee sales representative under Edward Gosling (son of C.G. Gosling, the former MD). He recalls a large sales force, including six reps for Greater London alone and thirty for the rest of the country, and a busy Export department. Hilary Shanahan, the agent for Eire, won the highest export orders, and Chris Petken the North London rep had the highest UK sales figures.

In 1975 Ivor Boyes retired and Tony Gray replaced him as Managing Director of Brettles – the second time he had been promoted into Ivor Boyes' shoes. Tony was replaced as Merchandise Director by Graham Newton, who had been Menswear Merchandiser. In September Gary Spendlove became the sales rep for the Midlands area, then in December 1976, as part of a swap, he moved and became the rep for Central and Southern Scotland.

Long Service Awards, New Bath Hotel, Matlock, 1975, includes Glen Hartshorn 58 years old, 43 years with Brettles, *Courtaulds News* August / September 1986.

Courtaulds Presentations outside the Belper canteen, 1979.

Sales to the Middle East

In 1975, the first comprehensive trade mission to the Arabian Gulf took place between 18th October and 13th November, promoting the forthcoming Spring & Summer 1976 range. It was a joint effort by 'the six member companies of the Courtaulds Wholesale Division', comprising Brettles Sales, Bradbury Greatorex, Batho Taylor & Ogden, Samuel Farmer, I. & R. Morley and M. Duke & Sons. Together, representatives went to Kuwait, Abu Dhabi, Dubai, Sharjah, Doha, Qatar, Oman, Bahrain and Saudi Arabia – a gruelling 36-day tour indeed. It cost £3,900 and brought firm orders totalling £127,509, a good start. The report, compiled just four days later by T. Hollingworth, L.H. Collins and W.O. Thorpe, stated:

> Sales achieved on any sales visit to this area will inevitably vary according to the order of visiting customers in relation to our UK competitors. Because of the number of different states to be visited, we might be first in one state, but will follow competitors like Martin Emprex and Cumberland Fashions in the next. To achieve any continuity of success, regular visits must be made to the area twice a year.[2]

In other words, the prosperity of the region was such that it was not necessarily price sensitive, and orders were likely to be placed with first comers. In any case, the report proved persuasive, and further group missions followed twice yearly.

A second trade mission to the same countries took place in 1976, between 27th February and 19th March. This time, while costing only slightly more, at £4,040, it took credit for a massive £305,237 of orders. The report five days later, again by Hollingworth, Collins and Thorpe, added that the contacts made on the first visit had 'led to many direct visits to our various showrooms and orders placed'. Courtaulds sales agents in the area were Messrs Spinneys, and it was at their showrooms that the products were displayed. However, the leaders of the trade mission were not completely happy with the support offered by Spinneys on the mission itself. The report complained that they were not once met off a plane and were only once given transport; this was to be corrected in the future. The report recommended that on large missions in future the representatives would divide into two teams, combining someone from each company, and each team would visit half the region – seemingly a more efficient and less exhausting method, which was subsequently followed.[3]

Later that same year, a smaller tour was made between 30th September and 22nd October, just to Saudi Arabia, Yemen and Libya. The tour cost £3,296 but only generated sales of £144,119. It would seem that the company were a little slow to adjust to cultural variations when engaging in Middle East sales, and the report, by N.A. Henderson and W.O. Thorpe, rather amusingly concludes: 'We feel that certain items can be excluded from future missions: Ladies' swimwear, Ladies' tennis dresses and skirts – no response at all. Ladies' nightwear – a smaller range to be carried' (!).[4]

Slump and Response

In 1979/80 the company saw a slump in UK business, and Courtaulds' top management required staff cuts. Tony Gray as Managing Director had made a point of getting to know all his staff and he used to do a shopfloor walkabout twice a day. He was now required to make a third of them redundant, which he remembers as a very painful experience. There were 38 redundancies, whilst several of the smaller departments were merged or closed.

In an effort to boost trade over the next two years, key departments launched new brand names – St Trop (swimwear), Gina Minetti (leisurewear), Niteline (nightwear) and Top Drawer (underwear) – all of which were successful. The Sales Managers co-ordinated the launch of their new ranges.

It would seem that the Courtaulds group also sought to improve efficiency further by centralising and combining the export activities of more of its companies, in joint missions. So on 19th May 1980, an Export Meeting was held at 'Courtaulds Distributors in Birmingham', to which were also invited 'Mr K. Senior, Export Manager of Brettles, and Mr D. Kellard, Sales Director of Morleys'. The meeting considered the relative success of various product lines, and concluded childrenswear and ladies' dresses had made a 'successful contribution' to the recent trips, but lines that required improvement were Brettles nightwear and Dukes skirts, and that there was a shortage of boyswear.[5] The autumn of that year saw a combined mission between 16th and 24th September to North Yemen, Bahrain, Saudi Arabia, Jordan and Egypt.

Courtaulds Hosiery (the manufacturing side) had abandoned the 'George Brettle & Co.' name in the early 70s. Outside Courtaulds, however, the name had been well respected, while that of 'Brettles Sales' meant nothing to the public. So by 1980, the old company name was reborn; Brettles Sales, as the sales and distribution arm, became the new George Brettle and Co. Ltd!

During the early 1980s, some Brettles staff were moved to other Courtaulds subsidiaries, and especially to Blount & Co. on Spencer Road or to Aristoc at Langley Mill.

The Stevenson Years

In 1981 by mutual agreement there were several director changes. Tony Gray chose to revert to the position of Merchandise Director, to specialise in his main strength. Gwyn Stevenson, who had worked for Courtaulds for 25 years, was brought in as Managing Director – and found himself locked in when wages were delivered on his first day! Gwyn had started his career in the lace industry in Nottingham and trained in lace manufacture at the Nottingham College of Art, then in Textiles and Management at Trent Polytechnic. He had joined Courtaulds in 1962 as Factory Manager, then Computer Project Manager, and progressed quickly to Administration Director, when he was involved in management training. He later became Managing Director of Holts of Leeds, then of S. & J. Watts of Manchester, whose offices are now the Britannia Hotel (both subsidiaries).

Also in 1981, a new showroom, designed by Derek Wingfield, was opened to attract buyers to visit and select their ranges. Derek had worked for years as the Lingerie department 'first man', Assistant Buyer then Menswear Merchandise Manager. The new showroom included a company museum, and both visitors and new staff found this very informative. Derek also played a major part in the growth of the factory shop on the A6.

Gwyn was a keen promoter of exports and extended Brettles sales to the Far East – Japan, Hong Kong and Taiwan. In particular he spearheaded the selling of woollen garments to department stores in Ginza, Tokyo, the most prestigious shopping centre in Japan. In 1987 he led a sales visit to Shanghai and Shenzhen in China. Gwyn was impressed by the efficiency and low cost of some Chinese producers despite the poor surrounding infrastructure, but was taken aback to find the army influencing their production decisions, a feature of the communist control economy.

Gwyn was also active in advancing European sales, and took exhibition space at the Salon de la Lingerie in Paris and elsewhere. Convinced that the reason many British companies struggled with exports was language barriers, he learned French, German, Italian and Danish and a smattering of Japanese. His belief in British exports went beyond Brettles, and in 1985 he became Chairman of the Intimate Apparel Committee of the British Knitting and Clothing Export Council.[6]

A list of the sales to various countries in 1984 has survived. The company exported to 31 countries that year, and some of the figures are particularly impressive. At the top of the scale, they exported £95k to Ireland, £85k to Saudi Arabia, £63k to Kuwait and £48k to Bahrain. It must be remembered that today's equivalent figures would be three or four times greater.

London Activities

Around this time, the permanently staffed London showroom at 48 Conduit Street, which had been managed by Sidney Foster, moved to 10 St George Street, still in Mayfair, under the management of Patricia Brooke. Patricia became somewhat famous, as Sarah Ferguson, the future Duchess of York, worked next door in number 11. Consequently Pat, at the front of the showroom, found herself filmed on national news for days on end, and wore a bright red jumper in order to stand out on television!

The showroom was well supported by retailers and became very important to the company. The main seasonal collections were launched there, as well as special promotion events. Carole Hunt, who was based in Alfreton, was always involved in and gave energy to the

London events. Carole's daughter Erica, a professional dancer, also worked as a Brettles showroom model for major sales events. There were also area shows in major UK cities and towns, including Belfast, Glasgow, Newcastle, Leeds, Cardiff, Bournemouth and Norwich.

The showroom in St George Street was just round the corner from Courtaulds' London headquarters in Hanover Square. The lease on this prestigious building cost £56,000 per annum, though this burden was reduced by sub-letting the ground floor to Sotheby's auctioneers. Gwyn Stevenson and Gary Spendlove were regular visitors to both buildings, and have vivid memories of one major sales event at Courtaulds headquarters, when a piece of scaffolding fell from a crane through the glass roof of their meeting room, causing injury to several colleagues from flying glass. One customer, Jan Tyrrell from Frillies of Horley, was quite badly injured whilst eating lunch.

Wood Street Showroom pictures

Showrooms at 48 Conduit Street
W1, based in London's Mayfair.

1985/6 Events

The years 1985 and 1986 saw more structural and management changes. In 1985 George Brettle & Co, became part of the 'Brands Group', also embracing Cooke and Watts. John Simpson was appointed as Sales Director, and the following year Mike Moulds joined the company as Financial Director. Graham Newton was then the Warehouse Director.

In the winter of 1985/6, severe icy weather over the Christmas holidays caused the sprinkler system to freeze and consequently burst. Employees returning to work after the holidays found the building flooded. Structural damage and loss of damaged stock was considerable, and many departments had to be relocated while extensive repairs were carried out. Syd Clarke recalls:

> After the Christmas hols I arrived with the security man at 7am, and noticed the north side of the main building was covered in thick ice, like a frozen waterfall. When we entered at the rear of the building we could hear the rush of water pouring out of the sprinklers inside, but as the water hit the outside it froze solid! We didn't dare to switch any electrics on, as we might have had an explosion. So after getting in touch with our 'top brass' and the fire brigade, we retired with the post to a safer and dryer part of the building. We reported to higher staff members, some of whom soon arrived including Gwyn Stevenson the Managing Director and other directors to help sort out a real mess.

The bicentennial year of the brand was celebrated in 1986, as it was 200 years since the term 'House of Brettle' had been coined by George Brettle's father, then trading as E. Brettle & Co. in London (although of course the true predecessor to George Brettle & Co. Ltd was the partnership of Ward Brettle & Ward, which was formed in 1803).

A dinner dance was held at the Swallow Hotel in South Normanton for all employees to celebrate the occasion, at which a commemorative mug was presented to all. An impressive cake was made modelled after the Belper factory, complete with bushes and trees, all edible! The *Belper News* produced a special 12-page 'Brettles Supplement', including congratulations from firms all over the East Midlands and a potted history which has been a useful source of information.[7]

BiCentenial Celebration with Factory Cake.

Bicentenary *Belper News* Brettles Supplement, 1986.

Move To Alfreton

However, the following year, 1987, after 184 years in Belper, Brettles had to leave their home town. Courtaulds decided to sell the site, which raised £750,000, and relocated the company to modern leased premises at Alfreton, eight miles to the north-east. The employees were not happy about it, but most were willing to travel. The Duke of Devonshire officially opened the 'new' Brettles building. At the same time the company was computerised, and as a result was able to streamline its operations. Despatch, packing and total staff were fewer in number than in the Belper days.

The original Belper factory shop, sited in Brettles yard, had been for employees only and was mainly an outlet for hosiery seconds. Under the management of Joy Southern and Blanche Lambert, the offer of merchandise at the shop had increased and so had turnover. In the early 1980s, the shop had been taken over by the Wholesale division (Brettles Sales), moved onto the main A6 and opened to the public, which had greatly assisted the growth of retail business. When the main business moved to Alfreton, the shop relocated to the Derbel building opposite the main Brettles building, and manager Blanche Lambert retired. Under the management of Derek Wingfield and the merchandising skills of Mary Pugh, the shop continued to be an important part of the business.

M Moulds,
G Newton, J S Taylor,
G Stevenson,
D S Wingfield,
R A Gray at Meadow
Lane Alfreton.

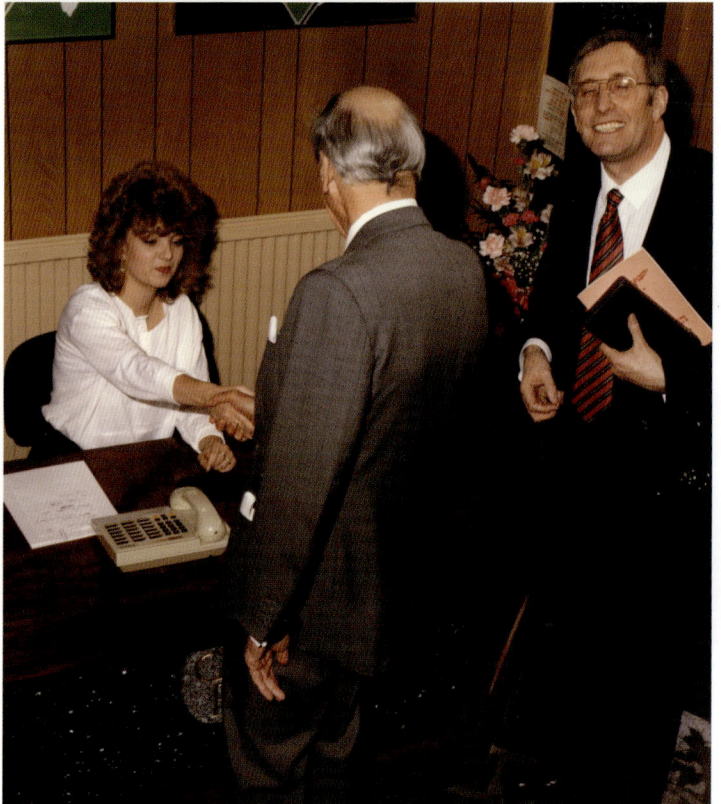

Duke of Devonshire visits
Brettles to open new Building,
Alfreton (also showing Gwyn
Stevenson), 1987.

Above: Outside Brettles Offices, Meadow Lane, Alfreton, late 1980s (Mike Moulds, Graham Newton, Gwyn Stevenson, Tony Gray, GS).

Left: Front of Brettles Warehouse, Meadow Lane/Salcombe Road, Alfreton, late 1980s.

Right: inside Brettles Warehouse, Meadow Lane/Salcombe Road, Alfreton, late 1980s.

Brettles Christmas Parties, 1970s.

Gwyn Stevenson presenting an original watercolour picture to Sandy Taylor.

Brettles Letterheads

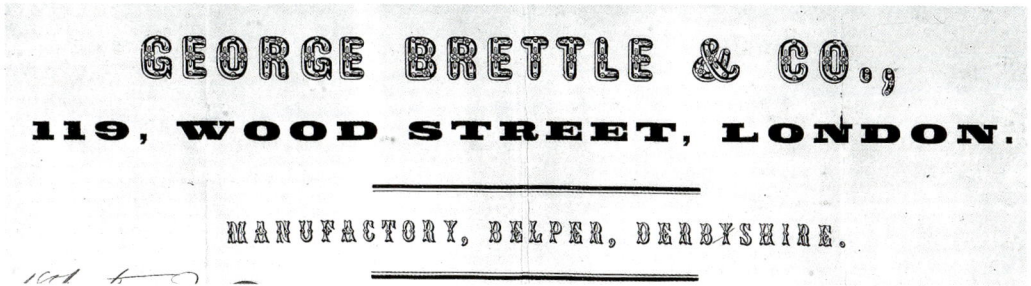

GEORGE BRETTLE & CO.,

119, WOOD STREET, LONDON.

MANUFACTORY, BELPER, DERBYSHIRE.

1869 letterhead.

TELEGRAMS: "BRETTLE, BELPER"

BRANDED GOODS:
"BELNIT" RIBBED UNDERWEAR
"OBERON" HOSIERY & UNDERWEAR
"LUSTRINIA" "SILKESTIA" "GLEAM"
"GLOSOSE" AND "SUNDENE"

TELEPHONE: 70 BELPER

GEORGE BRETTLE
& CO. LTD.

MANUFACTURERS OF
HOSIERY & UNDERWEAR

BELPER, DERBYSHIRE
18th December 1937.

1937 letterhead.

Brettles

Meadow Lane Alfreton Derby DE5 7EZ
(0773) 520400 Fax: (0773) 836439 Telex: 94011434 PW 413 Ext: 124

1989 letterhead (Photographer : Nick Locket).

Increased Sales and Exports

The company continued to expand, and very prestigious stores became important customers, including Harrods, House of Fraser, Fenwicks, Fortnum and Mason, Owen Owen, Beatties and Beales, all of whom were stocking a variety of Brettles merchandise. The use of the Wolsey brand, with its royal warrants of Her Majesty the Queen and the Queen Mother, also added to the quality image of the business and opened more doors with specialist retailers and new export markets.

Export growth also continued, with merchandise being shipped to over forty countries worldwide. Gwyn Stevenson and John Simpson won substantial orders from various Middle and Far East countries. The Middle East potential expanded, with demand from the UAE (Abu Dhabi and Dubai), Bahrain, Kuwait, Libya, Oman, Qatar and Saudi Arabia. Brettles merchandise was available in many top stores in most of the oil-rich Arabic countries, and these customers bought the quality 100 per cent cotton items. Trading in these markets was profitable, but less consistent due to fluctuating oil prices, the generally volatile situation and various conflicts in this area in the 1980s and 90s. Branded high-quality underwear also found favour in the lucrative Japanese and Taiwanese markets.

In fact, by the end of the 80s the company had sales agents in 45 countries, over three times as many as forty years earlier. The newer countries to which they exported included the USA, West Germany, Greece, Finland, Iceland, Lebanon, Syria, Jordan, Cyprus, Malawi, Malaya, Bahamas, Iraq and the Falkland, Faroe, Canary and Pacific Islands as well as past and present British territories such as Gibraltar, the Channel Islands, Hong Kong and Singapore. The company also developed trade in the nearer-to-home European markets, with many new customers.

Left: Severely damaged Beirut customer's retail outlet, 1982.

Right: GS and Mike Meredith, Kuwait Sheraton Hotel, 25th February 1983.

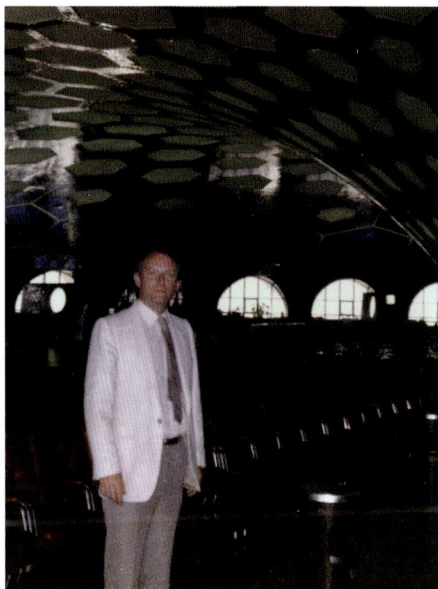

Left: GS with UK Ambassador and Business Attache, Kuwait. **Right:** Bev Cruikshank at Abu Dhabi Airport, 1987.

Left: GS at Emirates / Oman border, 1988.

In the UK, up to forty regional shows were organised each season, with the London and Belfast events usually producing the top figures. The permanent London showroom on George Street, still managed by Patricia Brooke, moved again to Margaret Street, adjacent to that of Courtaulds brands Aristoc and Gossard, and remained important to the export and large account business.

Meanwhile at Alfreton, the sales staff used the Haddon and Chatsworth showrooms to display their new collections to retail customers. These rooms were also used as meeting rooms for the staff. Conferences at various local hotels were a bi-annual event of the company calendar. The Makeney Hall Hotel in Milford was one of the most popular venues. These conferences were an opportunity for staff and agents to meet and discuss the new season's collections as well as sales performance.

A gradual decline in the numbers of the middle-market independent retailers allowed a reduction in the sales force. Despite this, the efforts of contract and key account managers Mike Meredith, Don McLeish and Chris Ham sustained and increased overall company turnover. The merchandise teams were constant in their innovative designs, which allowed them to keep pace with the ever more demanding customers. Tony Gray as Merchandise Director, Bob Ash as Lingerie Buyer and the team worked hard to ensure the company maintained its 'cutting edge' image.

Above: Maria Erith with Brettles Roadshow merchandise.

Right: GS with Robin Murcell, Sales Director of I. & R.Morley, and Mike Franklin, Sales Manager of Courtaulds Distributors, later Dukes Sales Manager.

Below: Dukes Sales Force and management team.

Above left: Derek Wingfield, Gwyn Stevenson & Sandy Taylor at Alfreton (by kind permission of Mervyn Spencer, Field Photographic of Heanor).

Above: Princess Anne with John Simpson, Gary Spendlove & Gwyn Stevenson.

Left: Princess Diana visits Belper and talks to Brettles staff.

Organisational and Management Changes

Meanwhile on the bigger canvas, the Courtaulds group split into two – Courtaulds PLC including cellulose and plastics, and Courtaulds Textiles, which of course included George Brettle & Co. There was no longer a Courtaulds Distributors Ltd. Brettles then acquired the Dukes Separates brand – an important acquisition. With it came some very experienced staff with strong backgrounds in sales and design. With Jill Regan as Merchandise Manager and Mike Franklin as Sales Manager, the Dukes team developed its new fashion range 'Imogen', which, with a very profitable scarf, glove and accessory business, quickly added over two million pounds to annual turnover.

In 1993 Gary Spendlove, after just 18 years with the company, was promoted to Sales Director to take the place of John Simpson, who had left to become Managing Director of Laura Ashley. The same year saw the retirement of Tony Gray, and his place was taken by Bob Ash, who was promoted from Merchandise Manager in the Lingerie department to Merchandise Director.

Three years later another old-timer retired – Syd Clarke the Accountant. Syd was the company's longest-serving employee, having joined in 1951, straight from the RAF, as a

Wages Clerk in the 'Counting House'. He had continued in Accounts and Finance for the next 45 years.

The Brands

It would be appropriate to mark the mid 90s by a brief resumé of the large number of brands owned and sold by the company. In alphabetical order, these were:

Bairnswear – a Courtaulds brand used only on a collection of school knitwear.

Brettles – the original brand, already described in the foregoing and earlier chapters of this book.

Dukes Separates – acquired by the company from the Birmingham-based Courtaulds distributor. Dukes contributed approximately 35 per cent of the company turnover in the 1990s.

Gina Minetti – invented by Brettles management and used to expand the casualwear offer in the 1980s and 90s.

Hussar – a brand invented in-house and used only on menswear.

Imogen – a fashion brand created by merchandiser Jill Regan and her team as part of the Dukes Seperates operation. Imogen was a collection of quality co-ordinates.

Kayser – renowned high-quality underslips and lingerie. Satin nightwear was very strong in the 70s and 80s.

Meridian – a brand used to supplement the men's and ladies' underwear department. Meridian also complemented the men's socks offer.

Morley – one of the oldest brands used in the business, formerly owned by I. & R. Morley of Heanor. The brand was used very successfully on a profitable scarf and gloves collection.

Niteline – using a telephone logo, Niteline was part of a vibrant young sleepwear collection in the 1970s and 80s.

St Trop – this brand enhanced the company swimwear collection and was used expansively to increase export turnover.

Vedonis – the warm underwear and cotton selection was a large part of the company's success in ladies' underwear. The brand still currently enjoys wide distribution in department stores and mail order catalogues.

Walker Reid – previously used with more mature ladies underwear, and re-launched in 2004 as a brand of exclusive high quality pure cotton nightwear.

Wolsey – the royal appointments of the Queen and Queen Mother were a great advantage on the high-quality underwear and knitwear. Paula Hamilton modelled a very exclusive collection using the Wolsey brand.

Brettles Brand

1989 Brettles Lingerie/Nightwear
Summer range.

Elegance in white from
Imogen Collection.

1989 Brettles Lingerie/Nightwear
Summer range.

1989 Brettles Summer range.

1991 St Trop Swimwear/Leisurewear Summer brochure.

1996 Brettles Lingerie/Nightwear Summer range.

'The Brettles Collection' (Gina Minetti, St Trop, Top Drawer, Nightline).

Brettles trademark & addresses on brochure.

Patricia Brooke and Beachwear Collections at 10 St George Street W1.

Dynamic modelling of new Wolsey underwear.

St Trop

Left: 1987 St Trop swimwear models.
Above: St Trop display stand at Swimwear Show, Olympia, 1990.

113

Imogen

Smart City-Girl look.

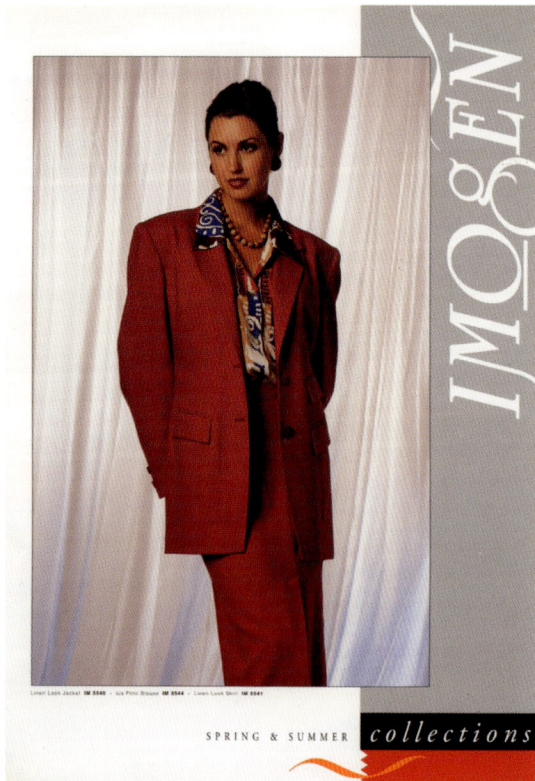

1996 Imogen Summer brochure.

Vedonis

Finesse Thermal Camisole, Vedonis brochure.

Wolsey Underwear
Modelled by top model Paula Hamilton

Wolsey Elegance in Pure Wool

Pure Cotton

THE DUBIED COLLECTION
IN 100% PURE COTTON
WD1418 LONG SLEEVE SPENCER
WD1416 PANTEE
FINE GAUGE SEAMLESS
GARMENTS WITH
DELICATE FEMININE
PATTERNING

Wolsey
L A D I E S W E A R

MEADOW LANE, ALFRETON, DERBY DE55 7EZ
TELEPHONE: 0773 520400 FAX: 0773 836439

LONDON SHOWROOM
13/14 MARGARET STREET, LONDON W1N 7LE

Wolsey brochure showing seal of
Royal Patronage.

From Courtaulds to Chilprufe

The 1996 accounts show Brettles with £711.7k net profit (16.5 per cent) on £4.3 million turnover, and Dukes at £169.8k net profit (8.5 per cent) on nearly £2 million sales. In any group, the net profit of an individual company depends on the way in which costs have been attributed, and on management charges, so it is perhaps more meaningful to note that the gross profits for the two brands were 34.5 per ent for Brettles and 29.4 per cent for Dukes. (Imogen sales had risen from £266k in 1992 to £962.6k in 1996, but no profit figure is given.) But by all available comparisons, Brettles was looking healthy.

By 1996, however, the Courtaulds group, like many others, was consolidating and concentrating on its core business, and discarding or selling off product lines now seen as peripheral to this. Courtaulds now identified hosiery as 'peripheral' and proposed to shed it.

In late 1996, six of the Brettles senior management team offered to purchase the company from Courtaulds Textiles and were expecting to commence trading as a privately owned independent business. But, unfortunately for the buyout team, at the eleventh hour a substantial offer was made by Leicester underwear manufacturer, Chilprufe Ltd, which was accepted by Courtaulds' main board of directors. The takeover was considered a move that would enable Chilprufe's collection of brands to potentially dominate the British knitted underwear market. Chilprufe already owned the White Swan trademark, so the acquisition made them a major player in the market sector.

Thus at the end of 1996 George Brettle & Co. became part of Chilprufe Ltd. Most of Brettles' staff were offered continued employment at the Meadow Lane site in Alfreton, some were moved to the Evington Valley Road factory in Leicester, while others were offered and took redundancy.

Many aspects of the Chilprufe experience were considered very positive by the former Brettles employees. These included a variety of import and export experiences, and included first visits to the Far East for some. The exposure to direct production (which few remembered) and the pressures of large-scale Far East manufacturing was again a new experience for many, although individuals recall being under considerable pressure when trying to keep the factories busy and also satisfy the demands of major accounts. But perhaps of greatest benefit were the relationships formed within the business that would prove mutually beneficial in the near future.

At first, the Brettles business continued to function as previously. After several management meetings, however, it became clear that the Brettles brand would not be part of any long-term Chilprufe strategy, and could possibly be phased out. It seemed that Chilprufe had no wish to expand the brand into the new millennium, and the name became less obvious in the marketplace. Some former Brettles management and staff, including Gary Spendlove, were not comfortable with the changing scenario and the new management style, and negotiated redundancy.

The Brettles Shop

Gary Spendlove ceased employment with Chilprufe on 31st October 1997. As part of Gary's redundancy package he acquired the George Brettle retail shop on Chapel Street in Belper, which came complete with staff members Mary Pugh, Sue Brindley, Mary Gould and Rachel Hall. This valuable asset, which was originally in the factory yard, had expanded and moved over the road into the building that had formerly been the manufacturing unit of Derbel Textiles. The extra floorspace had allowed a much wider selection of merchandise to be offered, which resulted in a substantial increase in turnover. Apparently a Llandudno coach company ran a regular trip to the Belper factory shop, as well as the new De Bradelei retail outlet which was situated in the former Brettles main three-storey building, and was also becoming very popular.

Although the Brettles Shop was in a poor condition in parts, it enabled Belper people to continue to buy Brettles produce, and also provided a secure and accessible building from which to start a new design, development and production company, Slenderella.

Meanwhile, back at Alfreton, the site closed at the end of 1999 and operations were moved to the Leicester site. The majority of staff now accepted redundancy, with just a few moving to Leicester. Just two years later, Chilprufe Ltd would go into receivership at the beginning of 2002, which could easily have been the end of the Brettles story. But it was not.

8. THE SPORTS AND SOCIAL CLUBS

Brettles had always provided for the social and recreational needs of its employees in various ways. Old ledgers indicate the purchase of sports equipment in the early years of the nineteenth century.

By 1850 they had established a library at 119 Wood Street, a debating society, a cricket club and a football club.1 Over the years many enjoyed the sports matches, the club dinners and suppers, the London trips to Gilbert & Sullivan operettas and other attractions. The earliest photographs are of the 'Oberon Cricket team' in 1858. Gary Spendlove writes (with tongue in cheek) that apparently the qualification for a plum job with Brettles was not a university degree or exceptional clerical ability, but a good 'right arm spin' or the skill to see off the pace attacks.

The origins of the term 'Oberon' are a little uncertain, but even in the late nineteenth century the firm was producing an 'Oberon' brand of ladies' and gents' underwear alongside the Brettles brand. The exact date of the founding of Oberon Athletic Club is also difficult to determine, but at some point it seems the 'Brettles Sports & Social Club' became 'Oberon Athletic Club' or 'Association', an umbrella for the various clubs and teams. In 1900 it was recorded that C. Broughton, Manager of the Worsted department, donated £300 and R. Carvery, the Assistant Manager, £165 to the Oberon Athletic Club. But the fact that the 15th AGM was held in 1934

Above: Oberon second eleven Football team, 1908.

Left: Brettles Cricket team, 1910 (Front: Mr Pollett, Dick Martin ; Middle: Redfearn, Dover, McKenna, Sperrin, Claude Noakes ; Back: Randall, McCassidy, Abderson, Kirkbridge, Sampson, Kendall.

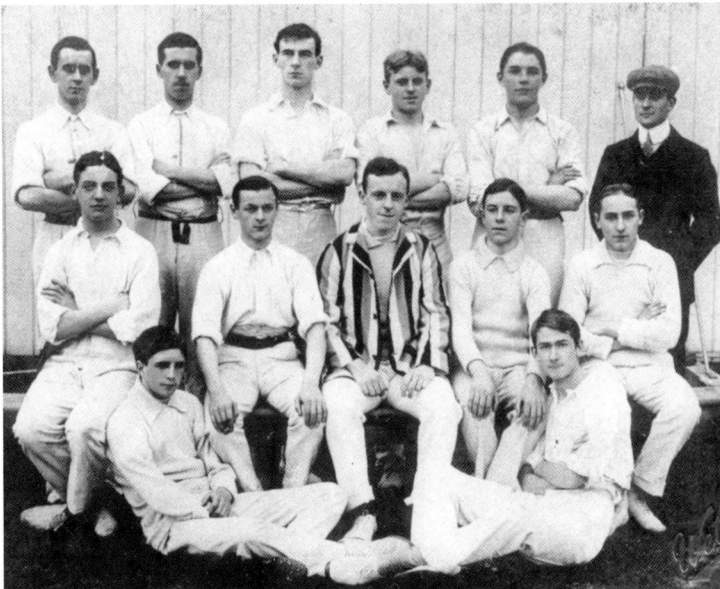

suggests that the club had been formed in 1919. On the other hand, the first edition of Yarns magazine in 1929 indicates that the score books of 'all Oberon Cricket matches since 1850' were extant.2

Prior to the First World War, it seems that the sports club went from strength to strength; the Brettles warehouse and factory were able to field three football and cricket teams, and had a full season's programme of fixtures, including shooting, tennis and crown green bowls. A notable pre-war Oberon athlete, W. Browse, was sadly killed in action at Ypres, and a solid silver memorial shield, standing an incredible 30 inches high, was presented to the club in his honour – the Browse Shield. For the next few decades this trophy was much coveted and was won by various individuals and teams. One of the last winners of the trophy was Ivor Boyes, who was to finish his career as Managing Director in 1975.

The Browse Shield, commemorating WH. Browse, killed in World War One (Photographer : Nick Lockett).

The 1920s saw major improvements in Oberon's sporting standards, resulting in the cricket club winning the City of London Championship. A highlight of the season was the visit of the Nottinghamshire county cricket team to London Oberon's Preston Road ground. This team included the great Harold Larwood. Both London and Belper also had football teams, and each year the firm staged a Twyford Challenge Cup match between the two, held alternately at both locations.

The 1929 match was played at Belper on 2nd March, with G.H. Ross acting as referee; the London team were especially strong that year, and beat Belper 9-2. 'Tea' was provided to both teams afterwards in the canteen, and the cup was presented by Mr Bowness, the Belper factory manager. In his speech he was 'pleased to note that the visiting team had on each occasion been successful, and that Belper hoped to maintain the tradition at Preston Road (the London ground) next season'.

The London team returned home and went on to play in the 'City of London TAASA Junior Championships' at Eltham a week later on 9th March 1929. Here they were even more successful, beating 'City Albion' 5-0. As a result they were promoted to the Senior League the following season. H.E. 'Monty' Montauban, the Honorary Secretary, wrote in Yarns that he 'felt confident they could find a cosy corner at 119 Wood Street for the Senior Trophy'.[3]

By 1929, when the first issue of Yarns magazine was published, the Athletic Club was well established, with football, cricket, tennis, bowls, swimming and athletics teams at London, all mirrored at Belper. The record of the club is not continuous, however: we have reports in Yarns between 1929 and 1932, AGM reports and accounts between 1934 and 1969, with some years missing.

Above: Brettles Tennis Club, 1920s and **right** Belper Oberons v Waingroves at Belper, 23rd March 1929. (Back row: N. Fryer, H.W. Hill, Edgar Tucker, Dick Martin, E.L. Davies, L.C. Boydon. Front row: A.M. Boby, Dover, G.B. Mason, Claude Noakes, M. Hunt, Parsonage.)

Sports in the 1930s

The Belper team was less successful than the London one in those early days. In January 1930 a *Yarns* article honestly reported:

> Belper club have not had a very successful season so far, and have only won one game. We are a very young side at present, but with perseverance, we shall give a better account of ourselves in future years. We enter the new year in a hopeful and confident manner.[4]

And in 1930 Belper Oberon's cricket fixtures included games against Belper Meadows, Ambergate, Cromford, Darley Dale and Wirksworth, all local teams with a long history.

In 1931 a new sports ground was opened at Raynes Park in Wimbledon for the London employees, with a newly built pavilion, replacing the former ground at Harrow.[5] At Belper, an extensive sports ground existed between the factory buildings and the River Derwent.

On 27th August 1932 the first Oberon Sports Day or 'Gala Day' was held at the club's new ground in Raynes Park. It was reported that the long jump was won by 'Brake' at a commendable 20' 4" and the high jump by 'Boyer' at an also impressive 5' 7". Whilst Belper staff were present, the participants in the event seem to have been mainly London staff: the 'Inter-Floor Relay Race' was won by 'the Ground Floor' (of 119 Wood Street). As well as the various races and contests, there was a fairground, 'light music was broadcast from a loudspeaker' and the report reads: 'The innovation of a microphone gave quite a modern touch to the proceedings, and was very effective in ensuring that races started on time.' At the end of the day, the prizes were given out by Mrs A.M. Gibson (wife of a manager), and there was a dance in the evening – a good time was had by all.[6] Also the annual London–Belper football match was held there for the first time.

From 1934 to 1969 there is a record of some annual general meetings and financial statements of the Oberon Athletic Club, which have been useful in tracing its progress. The patron up to 1964 was Sir Harry Twyford and the President was A.M. Gibson. The Honorary General Secretary was changed every three years or so – it was Mr A. Frapwell from 1933 to 1935, Mr R. Skidmore from 1936 to 1938 and Mr C.E. Gunn from 1939 to 1941 – whilst the Chairman and most officials were changed every year.

Sir Harry Twyford, the Company Chairman, contributed great enthusiasm to the club. He insisted that, for all fixtures, the club blazer and cap should be worn. Some of these still exist (though admittedly, by the 1980s, squad members usually arrived on match days in faded Levis and T-shirts!).

The Belper version of the constitution in the 1930s provided that membership was open to all employees of George Brettle, all wives, and, oddly, 'members of St Swithin's Church in Belper', which was 'subject to approval of St Swithin's Institute Committee'. Member subscriptions were 10 shillings; 'Outside' members' subscription was 15 shillings for gents, 12/6d for ladies.

Throughout the 1930s, the Belper AGMs were held in the canteen in late January each year, and the following are some of the reported highlights of those years. In 1934, it was recorded that the Cricket section won more matches than ever before, and the appointment of a second eleven was felt to be justified. Also in 1934, the Tennis section entered the fourth division of the Derby & District League, and did well the following year, only losing one match. Consequently, in 1936 they entered the third division, and again did well, finishing in third place.[7]

We may often complain about the English weather in our own times, but this was also a frequent problem at Belper in the 1930s. In October 1930, the report of the cricket season lamented: 'The clouds wept so piteously on every occasion we presented ourselves on the greensward, that in the end, the players gave up the ghost and longed for sunny skies. Not a single match was played here after the holidays, and only three away.'[8] A year later, the report reads: 'The annual cricket duel with London was held at Belper in uncertain weather. The ground was really unfit for the match, but there was no option but to carry on.'[9] And the following year, 1932: 'The ground was flooded at the start, with several feet of water' – surely an exaggeration![10] Again in 1937 the London cricket and tennis teams came up to Belper on Whit Saturday, but 'weather made play impossible'. The visit was not entirely wasted however: it is recorded that all attended an evening dance in the River Gardens Pavilion, and had a Peak District tour on Whit Sunday.[11]

The income of the Belper Athletic Club reached a peak of £124/1/3 in 1934. Only £10 of this came from employee 'member subscriptions', £35/4/6d from 'Other subscriptions', with £3 from 'Sale of grass'. A lower recorded income was £114/16/0 in 1936.

In 1936 the football section won the 'Belper Nursing Cup'. The following year the Belper Oberons won the Belper & District League Cup, and defeated the London Oberon team 7-2 at the annual friendly match.

In 1935, two members of the bowls section won the League Bowls Cup, presented by the *Derby Express*. In 1937 the bowls team played in the second division of the Belper & District Bowls League, and won the championship for the first time. By 1938 the bowls team were playing in the South Derbyshire Association League, and won half the matches they played that year.[12]

In 1938 the football team played in the Belper & District Amateur Football League and were 'runners up in three competitions'. This year they drew 5-5 in the away match with the London Oberons.[13]

On 27th November 1938 the club held its 19th AGM. The Executive Committee consisted of five ladies and ten gents. It was recorded that the Chairman was H.A. Widowson, the Honorary General Secretary was R. Skidmore and the Assistant Honorary Secretary was A.M. Fragwall. Member subscriptions that year totalled just £5. It was recorded that the Belper members had travelled to London at the end of the Coronation week to play the annual matches, including football, cricket, tennis, shooting, swimming and bowls.[14] In 1939 a new section, table tennis, commenced. Also that year for the first time there was income from whist drives.

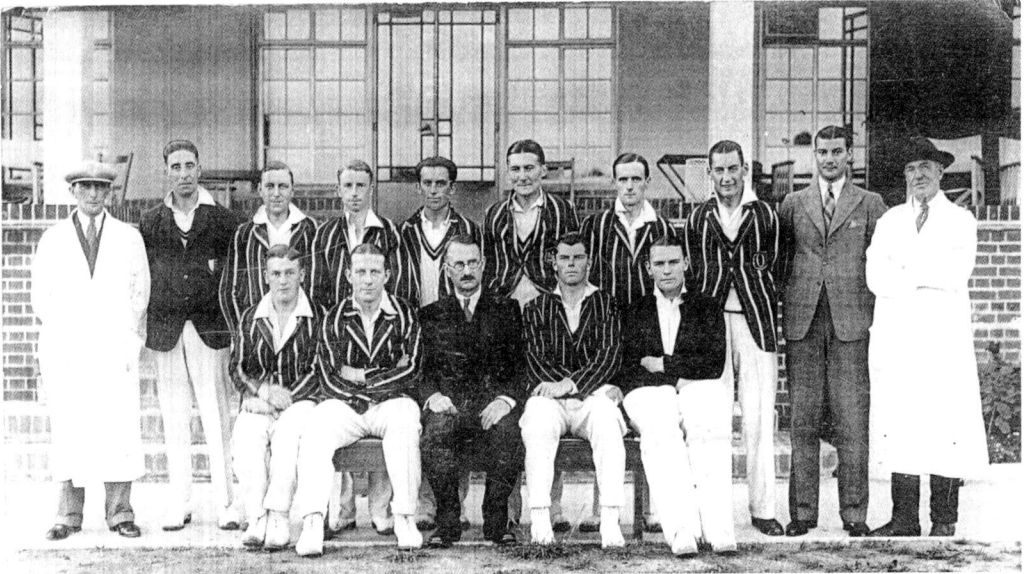

Above: Oberon First XI Cricket team with Harry Twyford, 1931. Winners of the City of London Textile AASA Senior Cricket Championship.

Left: Brettles' Oberon sports ground at Raynes Park, opened 1931.

Left: Sportsground opening ceremony, Chairman Harry Twyford speaking, 25th July 1931, with Kynaston-Stud.

Below: Oberon Football Team, 1st Eleven, London, 1931–2.

Left: Aerial view showing sports ground & Strutts drive to Bridge Hill House, *Derby Times*, 26th March 1932.
Right: Brettles Sports Day, 1930s, shows gasometer at rear left, since demolished.

Above: Sir Harry Twyford playing first bowl on new Oberon crown green.

Left: Large group including Tennis players in front of dyehouse on the Oberon playing field.

Below: Sir Harry Twyford with cricket team, London, 1930s.

Brettles Cricket Club, 1930s.

Brettles Men's Tennis team, 1930s.

Disruption of the War

The records of some of the war years are unfortunately missing. However, following the destruction of 119 Wood Street by bombing, most staff (or their jobs) were relocated to Belper, and the London Oberon club effectively ceased, as did most sports activities. The London sports equipment was relocated to Belper. In 1941 the accounts included 'Carriage for moving London equipment: £13/10/0', and also showed a donation to Derbyshire County Cricket Club of 1 guinea.[15] Thereafter, such records as we have are accounts for the combined club, all the remaining London staff having relocated to Belper apart from London travellers and a few clerks.

During the war, the number of sections functioning competitively varied from year to year. In 1941 there was only cricket and table tennis; in 1945, only cricket and bowls, though there was some expenditure that year on a new table tennis table and football equipment. Cricket was the only sport played every year throughout the war, with several old cricketers coming back to help out. The eldest, William Ross, aged 59, had 'come out of retirement', but topped the batting averages. Others were 57, 55, 53, and two aged 49. Despite this the team had done well, playing 18 matches, of which they won eight, drew six and lost only four.[16]

Less sport meant less expenses, and in 1944 it was recorded that the club was 'building up a substantial balance which we shall no doubt require when the war is over'.[17] They certainly did, and henceforth would need additional fundraising activities to supplement the subscriptions.

After the War

After 1945, returning servicemen renewed their membership subscriptions and the full repertoire of activities was resumed in the late 40s as finance permitted. By 1947 the workforce was mostly complete again, and members' contributions totalled £60. There were various further fundraising activities, though proceeds and profits varied. In 1947, two dances were held at the Derby Assembly Rooms, which made a net profit of £27/13/10d. On 13th February 1948 another dance at the Assembly Rooms sold 265 tickets, with proceeds of £35/2/6d, but too many costs were incurred and the profit was only 17 shillings. Christmas draws raised profits of £28/9/6d in 1949 and £12/19/4 in 1950. Whist drives that year raised £8/11/6, but a Beetle drive fell flat, raising only a shilling – presumably no more were arranged. The total annual club income including subscriptions rose to £353/12/0 in 1951, and to a magnificent peak of £957/12/1d in 1968.

From the 1950s onwards, there were two distinct entities – Brettles Sports Club, which played on Saturdays, and Oberon Athletics Club, which played on Sundays. After 1950, most football was played on Sundays, and was thus an Oberon activity. The other regular activities throughout the 1950s were, for Oberon, cricket, hockey, tennis and bowls, while basketball was played between 1950 and 1953. The Sports Club played football, bowls, tennis and table tennis (1968 accounts).

As for Oberon Athletic Club officials in the 1950s, we know from a *Derbyshire Advertiser* article that Charles Doerr replaced H.G. Randall as Secretary of the club and that P.A. Nash replaced W. Inch as Treasurer. Randall and Inch both retired from the company in 1959.[18]

Brettles Sports Day, 1950s including E. Flinders, Ginny Allen, Dorothy Allsop, Sarah / Elsie Greatorex, Jim Bowler & wife' and right 'Shooting game, Derwent Street buildings to rear, 1950s'.

Sports under Courtaulds

After the Courtaulds takeover in 1964, the constitution and rules of the 'Oberon Sports & Social Club' were updated. Its objects were stated to be, firstly, the 'provision of opportunities for recreation, social intercourse, refreshment, the playing of games and sports for the benefit of its members'. And secondly, 'the provision and maintenance of a clubhouse in George Brettle & Co. Canteen'. The next clause, as rewritten, stated that 'every ordinary member shall be an employee of Courtaulds Hosiery Division (Spencer Road and Chapel Street Belper factories)'.[19] 'Spencer Road' was the Blounts factory, which was combined with the main Brettles factory, along with that of Aristoc of Langley Mill, under Courtaulds. The sports club activities mostly continued unchanged.

A receipt dated 24th September 1969, under the letterhead 'Brettles Sports Club' of Chapel Street, Belper was for eight cups for that autumn, some sponsored by individual directors past or present. There was a 'Brettles Challenge Cup' each for cricket, tennis and bowls and a 'Gibson Challenge Cup' for cricket and tennis (Men's Open). There were two more cups for bowls – a 'Bowness Bowls Cup' and a 'Sir Harry Twyford Cup' – and also a 'Randall Challenge Cup' for tennis (Men's Handicap). Consistent with this, the 1969 minutes state that the tennis and bowls teams won three trophies each, and the cricket team two trophies, all in solid silver – all in all a successful year.[20]

Memories of the 1970s

In the 1970s Oberon Football Club started playing in the Alfreton & District Sunday Football League in the fourth division, and played local teams such as Heanor Athletic for the Leaderflush Shield.

Gary Spendlove, who joined Brettles in July 1973, was involved in sports from the start. He reflects:

> Sport was always on the agenda at Brettles. Football, cricket, bowls, tennis, netball and hockey all had competitive teams. The local leagues featured the football and cricket sides. The football teams played Saturday and Sunday games, although they were organised by totally separate committees. The Sunday team usually used the Oberon name, which is still used by five-a-side teams in local leagues today. In the 1970s, many of the staff played in the matches, although to enhance the performance of the sides, quality, local players from outside the company were 'imported'. The cricket team in the 70s and 80s acquitted themselves well in the well-organised Works League, at times winning the league and the cup. The unwritten rule was for the cricket side to field nine employees, with two other players having to be related to current staff, usually wives or parents.

Interestingly, the grassland to the west of the company site used for sports also had an army assault course used by the Herbert Strutt School combined cadet forces. Strutt's School also used the Oberon ground for cricket, football and hockey matches. The Oberon playing field also contained a large bowling green, three tennis courts, and high jump and long jump training areas.

Social events were well attended, including an appearance by Gary Glitter in a large marquee on the Oberon field in the seventies. The canteen was a popular venue for dances, discos and concerts. Punk rock band 'Robin Banks and the Payrolls' performed at high volume to a mixed and somewhat deafened audience. Peter Oakley is remembered to have organised some excellent events, and kept a well-stocked bar. Former employees remember enjoying a splendid pint of beer after matches.

Gary recalls the inter-department six-a-side competitions, and that the Sports section played darts, dominoes and table tennis. Brettles Sports & Athletics played football on Saturdays, and Belper Oberon Football Club (which included 'outsiders') on Sundays. Brettles Sports also organised ladies' football matches. The cricket team was organised by Peter Oakley, and played in the Belper and District Works League against teams from Lubrizol, Stevensons, Dyers, Richard Johnson & Nephew and Denby Pottery. There were also matches arranged between other Courtaulds factories. After the matches at Belper, a buffet and bar were provided and there was plenty of socialising all round.

The next surviving document is a letter dated 1st November 1977 from Stewart Wrightson

(UK) Ltd, insurance brokers to Brettles Sports Club, confirming personal accident insurance for members playing football, cricket or in the 'Girls' Netball Team'. This was itemised and Football cover was by far the most expensive, costing £3.42 per member whilst the others each cost under a pound.

In 1982 Andy Conkleton, an established player, became Oberon Football Club Manager, and a series of successes followed. That year they won the Kimberley Shield for the Division Four Championship, and were duly promoted to the third division. In 1983/4 they took third place in that division, and the following year they did even better and were promoted again. In 1985/6 they came third in the second division; the next year they did still better and were runners-up. Finally, in 1988/9 they entered Division One and again immediately achieved third place.

A small cluster of documents from the end of the eighties include a letter dated 8th June 1988 from Brian Clough to Gary Spendlove, responding to an invitation to attend the club's end-of-season dinner in July (unfortunately Brian was unable to oblige on that occasion). Belper Oberon's 1989/90 accounts show income of £421.22 from subscriptions, £43 from raffles and £89 from 'blackouts'. A special menu indicates that a Belper Oberon Football Club dinner was held at the Talbot Hotel in Belper on 20th July 1990, with main course choices of steak, scampi or chicken.

There are several insurance documents from around this period, showing how members were provided for. There is a Renewal Receipt from the Excess Insurance Company dated 15th January 1980 for £49.88. A 1981 renewal quotation letter from broker Stewart Wrightson London Ltd, quaintly handwritten, shows a Death Capital Benefit of £1,000 for football and cricket players and a Temporary Total Disablement Benefit of £10 per week. A similar letter ten years later, dated 27th September 1991, shows significant benefit increases – Death Benefit or Permanent Total Disablement £3,000; loss of one limb or eye also £3,000; Temporary Total Disablement £30 per week for up to 104 weeks.

By 1990, Gary Spendlove was the Chairman of Belper Oberon Football Club. A copy remains of Gary's message to members as Club Chairman. This was also the occasion of Andy Conkleton resigning as Manager after eight years, though agreeing to continue as a committee member. He had earned the thanks of the whole club. The message also indicates the fundraising activities that were going on at the time. These included sponsored walks, car rallies, raffles, a raft race, and the selling of 'blackouts'. The football team were then in the Alfreton Sunday League first division. Sunday home games kicked off at 2.15pm in Eyes Meadow, Duffield. Training nights started at 6.30pm at Belper Sports Centre.

In the late summer of 1996, as the company was changing hands, a cricket match was played on Belper Meadows between the Brettles and Chilprufe teams, at which David Wall of Chilprufe was considered to be 'man of the match'.

It is nostalgic to reflect back, but the heyday of the sports and social club may have been the 1920s and 1930s, when the company invested large sums of money in the Belper and London sports grounds. The Preston road sports pavilion alone would have cost around one million pounds in today's terms. It is also important to remember that the sports club were very strong after the Second World War, with most staff making a small financial contribution from their wages.

The Oberon or Brettles sports and social clubs do not exist today as they did in previous times, but the present company sponsors some local sporting and secular events, and staff take part in charity quiz events and organise the occasional dinner or luncheon, though physical sports are not usually on the agenda. The company does, however, currently operate a cricket coaching programme with schools and youth groups. The Oberon name continues to be used by local five-a-side football teams in the well-organised Belper leagues, although no current staff members are involved. The league is organised by former Oberon team manager Andrew Conkleton and goalkeeper Mark Green.

Above: Belper Oberon v Polygon (Alfreton), 19th October 1975 (Back row: Brian Cornfield, Will Gascoyne, Chris Bacon, David Earnshaw, Duncan Bennett, Malcolm Knapp, Karl Schmit. Front row: Peter Nightingale (Manager), Steve Gascoyne, Nigel Oldrini (Captain), Mick Phillips, Gary Spendlove.

Right: Miss Brettle early 1970s.

9. PERSONAL MEMORIES

The history covered in Chapter 7 spans over thirty years, taking us well into the period remembered by many former employees, and is dotted with many personal recollections. This chapter combines the more extensive memories of some former directors and others with long careers. The first of these comes from Gary Spendlove, owner of the current Brettles business and Slenderella. He joined the old Brettles company straight from school on 30th July 1973, and has extensive memories of that period.

Above: Front of Brettles Factory in the 70s, Chapel Street, Belper.

Left: Side of Brettles Factory in the 70s, Chapel Street, Belper.

Working in the Despatch Department

Like many school leavers and teenagers, I started work feeling well educated and quite worldly wise. My first day at Brettles despatch department changed all that. There were so many colourful characters with wonderful stories. Tales about the war, working 'down pit', moving the London side from London (what was that all about?), sports and social clubs. Plus many personal yarns of triumph and tragedy, so it was no small wonder that I was hooked on the Brettles story from day one. As my employment progressed I became aware of vague quotations about various kings and queens, the Lord Mayor of London, Nazi politicians, ambassadors, political leaders, and even about supplying Admiral Lord Nelson's underwear – in fact more, incredible history than you could seriously comprehend, and totally beyond the experience of a Belper lad. But on reflection, all those stories were based on serious fact, and were only 'the tip of the iceberg'.

My first position as a trainee sales rep was in the Despatch Department, which occupied the part of the factory which is now the De Bradelei factory shop. The Despatch Department consisted of four sections: A–E, F–N, O–Z and 'Town', which was for the London area customers. The various retail customers were allocated to the section by the initials of their town. So, for example, a customer at Bridgnorth would be in the A–E section, whilst Harrods, or Pearsons of Enfield, or Fairheads of Ilford would be in the Town section.

As well as the four sections, there was the Despatch Office with Denis Campbell as the manager. Well respected as a perfect gentleman and renowned for his polite efficiency, Dennis, along with his assistant, John Haggerty, ran a tight ship. A subsection of the Despatch area was the Packers, most of whom were splendid characters with incredible stories to tell of old Belper, World War Two, life in the coal industry or, as they used to say, 'down t'pit'. The 'Adrema', 'Flimsy room' and loading bay were the other areas. Being sent to the Flimsy room to ask for a 'long weight' (or 'wait', as it transpired) on one's first day conjured up a nervous time, especially when one of the female staff slid the door behind me and asked my requirements – I have always been a little claustrophobic in confined spaces. Smoking was only permitted in the toilets, so tea breaks saw a towering inferno of tobacco smoke erupting from the gents' toilets, where each smoker had his own cubicle to sit down!

I was perhaps sold the job by the then Personnel Manager, George Morley. George was a former football league referee and very much 'old school', considered by staff to be a stern disciplinarian. Although small of stature, he carried an impressive authority, ensuring no staff extended tea breaks when they heard the click-click of his steel-tipped brogues on the stone floors. In fact some of the ex-military staff were seen to stand to attention in his presence.

Shopfloor Memories of the 70s

There were many others in Belper who started work with Brettles at around the same time as Gary or earlier, and I have managed to speak to a number of them, each with their particular memories.

Geoffrey Futter joined Brettles in 1965, soon after the Courtaulds takeover, staying for seven years. He worked first on the Ladies' Underwear sales side, putting orders together. Geoff remembers that, in the Factory, the original long knitting frames had been replaced by tall Zodiac frames made in Italy. People he remembers well from those days are George Wyatt, a buyer, Norman Jepson, the reception doorman, John Nind in Yarns, Arthur Hill in the Knitting department and Jim Workman in the Dye House. Later Geoffrey worked in the Wages Office with Sid Clarke.

Geoffrey remembers the complete separation between the manufacturing side (the Factory) and the wholesale side, which was still referred to as the 'London side', since this work had originally moved to Belper from London in 1940. He confirms the continued elitism and that staff in the 'Counting House' serving the London side still felt superior to those in the Wages Office serving the Factory!

Geoff also remembers the staff meeting that was held in 1971 to discuss the introduction of decimalisation, and recalls with some amusement asking what on earth 7/6d would be in new pence, and commenting how difficult it would be to multiply this by three, etc. Geoff left in 1972 to work for Denby Pottery as a financial manager, but after an absence of 38 years, he joined the present Brettles–Slenderella company in February 2010.

Ian Farrell also joined Brettles in the mid 1960s and worked in the Warehouse on ladies' casuals, sweaters and jumpers. His boss was Ivor Boyes, who was a Buyer but later went on to be a Director, then Managing Director. Ivor's deputy was Maurice Shanahan.

Ian remembers the wooden temporary canteen in 1971, used while a new canteen was being built by contractors Bowmer & Kirkland, which was opened the following year. The canteen was used not only for normal lunches but also for evening events for staff and outsiders of a dinner-cabaret kind. Most of the performers were local singers or tribute bands, but on one occasion Gary Glitter was the star! Because of the numbers expected this was held in a marquee, though the success of the event was marred when a glass was thrown and hit Glitter on the head. Rowdiness, it seems, is nothing new. Ian left Brettles in 1974 to work in the Police Stores in County Hall, Matlock.

Among those I spoke to were the two Palmer sisters, who both started with Brettles directly from school at age 15, seven years apart, and both served the standard six weeks in training school before being placed in their respective departments. **Edie Palmer** started in 1964, and was employed in putting elastic on tights, then on toe seaming. **Pat Palmer** started in August 1971, and worked in the Toe Seaming department with her sister. She recalls that there were 40 to 50 staff in the department, and the senior ones 'mothered' the newcomers such as herself. They each worked with a sewing machine and a suction tube, into which the stockings were drawn, enabling the worker to 'run through the seam'. Sometimes a joker would reverse someone's airflow so that stockings flew up into the air! Their 'boss' at this time was Alice Watson.

Company policy for filling new departments was to transfer staff on the basis of 'last in first out', so that the most experienced were normally left in place. So when a new 'Straightening Room' was started, Pat joined the new team there. The work involved stretching stockings over a glass leg, then flattening and stacking them into dozens. The products then went to the Dye House, then to Folding and Packing. Each department had its dedicated mechanic for repairing its own machinery.

The Palmers remember the winter of 1972 with its strikes and the 'three-day week' of power supply. The biggest problem, however, was when on occasions the power suddenly went off without warning, and the workers were pitched into darkness. Pat remembers having to descend a ladder in the dark and the chill of hearing cockroaches crunch under her feet!

Pat left in 1975 to work for Flanders. Edie by this time was employed in putting labels on pantaloons and vests, and in elasticating briefs that were intended for Marks & Spencer. From the mid 1980s, some staff began to be transferred to Blount & Co, another Courtaulds subsidiary on Spencer Road (the building is now a nursing home). Edie Palmer was moved there in 1986, but found it a rather harsh regime, with individual output targets being continually raised without any increase in pay, and she finally left in 1989.

Pat Thawley joined Brettles in 1968 and was posted to the 'Entering Room' (customer names A–E). She enjoyed this work and stayed in it for nearly twenty years. Among Pat's memories are the 'RM' (Ready Money) days, when staff were allowed to visit other departments and buy sample stock cheaply. The move to Alfreton in 1987 was no problem to Pat as she lived in nearby Heage. She was moved into the Lingerie department there, where she 'pulled the orders', including bulk orders for Makro. As a part of this she maintained a stock of labels for all the regular customers, and used 'Adrema' stamps for printing the labels. She worked partly in the warehouse, dealing with both incoming goods and outgoing orders.

Sue Brindley joined Brettles in 1972 and was moved several times to give her a breadth of experience. She started on telexing and copying, then moved to the internal Post Office where she worked with June Butler and Maj Walters. She then moved to the Entering Room (customer names O–Z), working with Wilf Watson and Joan Gibb, and it was here she met Pat Thawley, with whom she was to work closely in future years. The next move was into the factory shop, at around the time when this went from being a company shop for staff to being a public shop facing onto the street. Working in the shop saved Sue from moving with most of the workforce to Alfreton in 1987. Here she worked with Mary Pugh and Mary Gold. The shop sold a number of brands besides Brettles, including Marks and Spencer seconds, and was frequently visited by whole coachloads of customers.

Pat and Sue remember several colourful characters from Brettles' Belper days. One was George Hawkins, a spiritualist who claimed to see ghosts in the factory and also that there was a 'Brettles in the sky' consisting of deceased employees. Another was George Morley, the Personnel Manager, who behaved as though he was everyone's line manager and was somewhat feared. Most of the factory jobs involved continuous standing; as there were no seats, staff sometimes took a couple of minutes to sit on their bench when opportunity allowed. If George then passed by, he would shout 'Get off that bench', which was instantaneously obeyed with a shudder.

The Departments in the 1970s and 80s

Gary Spendlove now describes the Belper departments in the 70s and 80s, which were oddly numbered from 71. Possibly the earlier numbers had been departments in London up to 1940, or perhaps there was a more subtle presentational reason!

Each of the six departments in the 1970s was managed by a Merchandiser or Buyer, who had often been an area sales representative, so the Department Merchandiser's position was seen as a definite career progression. Although the Brettles collections were generally of classic design, the merchandisers were very much 'on the ball' with cutting edge fabrics and designs. New brands such as Gina Minetti, St Trop swimwear and Niteline lingerie were all internal innovations, adding considerable intrinsic value to the company.

Department 71 was **Menswear**, where Graham Newton as Buyer developed fine collections of knitwear and underwear. The men's sock department, also known as Half-Hose, had a reputation for excellent quality. Some items were even sold with their own darning wool ball – remember the darning mushroom? A major customer was the Central Electricity Generating Board or CEGB. They would purchase considerable quantities of heavyweight 'sea boot hose', which were also sold to deep sea fishermen. The high-quality men's warm underwear enjoyed a wide distribution throughout the UK. The 'first man' in Menswear was the very able William 'Bill' Aldred. The staff there occasionally enjoyed an impromptu game of cricket, the 'pitch' located in the second aisle of the main walkway! Long-serving member of staff Glen Hartshorne excelled at his version of department spin bowling.

Department 72, **Hosiery**, was originally the cornerstone of the Brettles business. The company had historically produced silk hosiery for King George III and Queen Victoria. Also, specialist hosiery was previously made for various celebrities and sports stars, including size 16 socks for World Heavyweight boxing champion Primo Carnera. Examples of such items are on display at the Belper North Mill Museum.

Pure cotton hosiery contributed substantially to the hosiery offering. Syldene and Belsheen hose were sold to major retailers. Some of these items were retailing at over £12 a pair – quite a luxury when a pint of beer was selling for two shillings (or ten pence today).

The superfine 'Cheri' fully fashioned stocking enjoyed a renaissance in the mid 1970s, the pointed heel adding a sexy image. A collection of fishnet and Italian lace hosiery also gave the company a cutting edge over much of the competition. Lisle stockings were also dyed white and supplied for stage and film productions of *Mutiny on the Bounty* and *Les Miserables*. The colourful and energetic Mike Hayman was the hosiery buyer, with the ever efficient John Abbot as first man. Mike had previously been a traveller for the company in North Wales, as had his father.

Department 73 was the **Children's department**. Brettles childrenswear also had a reputation for top quality, with the famous blue and white boxes visible in many quality retail outlets. Pure cotton socks were a major part of the department's turnover. Arcadian, Charter and Dualwear were sub-brands in the sock department. The pure cotton and pure wool underwear also contributed to a highly successful business. The Merchandiser, Leo Collins, had been a cornerstone of the sales force, and added his skill to the buying team. Leo also contributed greatly to the company export turnover in the 1970s, especially with visits to the Middle East. Specialist items such as baby nests were exported in volume to the Arab countries and North Africa. The department's 'first man' was the very experienced Trevor Brown, again a long-serving member of the management team. Prince Charles was known to have worn Brettles socks as a boy, adding to the company's Royal connection.

Department 74 was the **Lingerie department**, and had a reputation for innovation with style, fabrics and colours. The 1970s and 80s saw many developments in yarns and satin polyesters, viscose and nylon, including 'tricoloop', featured in the twice-yearly collections. Packaging also played a major part in the image of the business. In fact some staff joked that the black and gold dressing gown boxes were more valuable than the item they contained! The Brettles slip or underskirt collections were in great demand. 'Anti-stat' nylon was a major seller, along with the polyester and Celanese items. Tony Gray was the Merchandiser in the

1960s and early 70s, and was very innovative with the nightwear and dressing gown collections, which included luxury satin-lined quilts, pyroseen and botany wool dressing gowns. After his promotion to Merchandise Director, he was succeeded as Merchandiser by another excellent former traveller, Doug Penton, who was later succeeded by Don Whewell. Department 'first man' was Derek Wingfield, who became Menswear Merchandise Manager following the promotion of Graham Newton to a directorship. As part of the Courtaulds Textiles Division, the Brettles team had access to many development facilities and the technology of a major international company, which along with the Courtaulds Chemical Division was listed in the *Financial Times* 100 top companies. Tom Alton followed Derek Wingfield as first man, upon promotion from the Woven Underwear Export Supervisor role.

Department 75 was **Woven Underwear**. Historically this department was a flagship for Brettles. The underwear had previously been made at Belper, but the strategy was to design, with the finished goods being made at other established factories like Hodgkinson & Gillibrand, Harrison & Hayes, Ellis's, Vedonis, Ratby Garments and others. The underwear offering was considered to be medium to high quality, with many natural fibres included. The addition of more unusual fabrics such as Orlon, Banlon Nylon and Courtelle all guaranteed a 'cutting edge' to this department and were an important part of the success under Buyer Michael Hayman. Mike had taken the reins after the retirement of long-serving Merchandiser George Wyatt, and again had been promoted from the sales force (and his father had also been a successful traveller with the firm). Mike's first man was the dedicated Derek 'Paddy' Powditch, who was always prepared to work overtime and go the extra mile for the company at peak times. Tom Alton worked very hard to look after the many export orders, while Jack Rooth, ex-submariner Derek Barnes, music-loving Steve Kerry, Trevor Spencer and Minnie Harrison were key members of a very colourful team. Sadly Mike Hayman died prematurely, which was considered a serious loss to the merchandise management team.

The Woven department also had a great team ethos, with 'all hands on deck' when large deliveries arrived. The arrival of the blue box from Vedonis of Hucknall on a Friday afternoon always gave the staff a thirst for their Friday night pint. It would involve putting many hundreds of one-dozen boxes from the van onto 'wheelers' then onto the goods lift for checking and fixturing. The order pickers would then pull the orders prior to despatch via the 'Entering Room'. Interlock underwear created a large part of the Vedonis collection, so moving this stock was physically demanding, due to the weight of the fabric. '2057D' and '7477D' were the top-selling Vedonis items, and the Brettles 'R1470' pure cotton group was the department's best seller. Other winners were the wool groups of Grace, Regal, R1605 and Supreme. The top customers for underwear at the time were the Binns group from Sunderland. The Portsea Island Co-op of Hampshire was another major customer.

But it wasn't all work and no play. It was common for some members of staff to play dominoes or cards in their lunchtime; three-card brag with its various connotations was a popular game. On occasions, World War III nearly erupted after one of the younger syndicate produced a 'run on the bounce' or a 'prile of threes'. There was deep pressure surrounding these games, with heated verbal exchanges; well, what do you expect when you are playing for a penny a life?

Gary remembers that in certain hard winters, and when there were power cuts, free soup in generous quantities was provided by the management. The department junior would be designated to do the canteen run for a large jug of pea and ham or minestrone soup.

Department 76 was the **Ladies' Casualwear** department, but also included school knitwear and swimwear. Although not the traditional Brettles image of hosiery and underwear, the ladies' fashions expanded through the 1970s and 80s, and 21-gauge fully fashioned knitwear sales formed a large part of the department turnover. The parent company yarns were used extensively with sales in Courtelle knitwear. Trevira also took a substantial market share. The additions of the 'Gina Minetti' brand along with the St Trop swimwear ensured the fastest growth area in the business.

The Casuals department was the most southerly of the Brettles buildings, being on the part of the site acquired from Wards. The porters in Casuals were considered the fittest in the company as all assets had to be taken across the car park in wheelers or trolleys. The department was adjacent to the company infirmary or sick room, complete with company nursing staff. Another former traveller, J.S. or 'Sandy' Taylor, was the Merchandiser during this period. Sandy was succeeded by Charles Andrew as the business moved to Alfreton. The long-serving first man was Maurice Shanahan, who was succeeded by Christopher Burrows.

The Melissa Bell swimwear collection caused a sensation in the 1990s and attracted considerable publicity in the national press. The collection was launched in the packed 'Hollywoods' nightclub at Romford, to a celebrity audience, and the company hired a luxury coach from Alfreton for the occasion. Melissa Bell played the character Lucy in the *Neighbours* TV series, and guests at the event included cast members of *EastEnders*, *Neighbours* and *Home and Away*!

Sales Representatives and Sales Areas in 1984

Area & Area No.	Sales Rep	Area & Area No.	Sales Rep
Northern Ireland (35)	L. Reid	West Midlands (4)	A. Unwin
Northern Scotland (37)	B. Spence	East Midlands (3)	G. Bailey
Central Scotland (30)	S. Burnett	East Anglia (11)	T. Purkiss
South Wales (29)	G. Bayley	Essex (42)	E. Daniels
Greater London (61)	P. O'Connell	Kent (10)	S. Perrin
Tyneside and South-East Scotland (5)			J. Haswell
Lancashire and Greater Manchester (7)			G. Spendlove
Yorkshire and Humberside (9)			J. Atkinson
Cumbria and South-West Scotland (20)			F. Blakey
North Wales and Merseyside (24)			R. Arrowsmith
Avon, Wiltshire and Berkshire (27)			A. Fitchett
Hampshire, IOW, Channel Islands (15)			A. Croucher
Cornwall, Devon, Somerset, Dorset (18)			K. Mortimer

Merchandising Memories

Tony Gray served Brettles for over 22 years from 1972, including 16 years as Merchandising Director and six years as Managing Director. The following are some of his memories from the 1980s.

Tony remembers leading several successful promotions that boosted wholesale sales. One of these was a 'National Knickers Week', with several special offers including a 'Baker's Dozen' offer of one free pair for every twelve pairs ordered, and a prize offered to retailers for the best window display, for which competition was fierce, and sales were significantly boosted.

Tony was very aware of the need to be fashion conscious in the range offered. He wrote a booklet for buyers and sales staff entitled 'Unravelling the Mystery of Underwear', in which he stated that 'Retail buyers tend to be very conservative in their buying habits where underwear is concerned. They will buy what they sold last year, but need to be persuaded to try new styles and new ideas.'

One of Tony's special strengths was networking and relationship building. He struck up productive working relationships with fellow directors, especially Gwyn Stevenson, the MD, with staff, with the Hosiery Workers Union representative (which served him well when 'talking down' a 25 per cent pay rise bid), and very importantly with suppliers. One of these was John Raven, whose company, Ratby Garments, was an underwear manufacturer and supplier to Brettles. They went on several joint trade missions to Germany and Holland together, with a team of ten buyers and sales reps.

Following the closure of a gloves manufacturer, Tony arranged for its whole stock, including leather gloves, to be purchased by Courtaulds and moved to their London showroom in Albemarle Street, thus increasing the range. He also added headscarves to the range, and after meeting various European manufacturers sourced these from Lake Como in Italy and from Czechoslovakia.

One of Tony's memorable successes was the purchase of 500 dozen Japanese printed squares at a price that enabled them to be sold back to Japan at a worthwhile profit! He was very successful at negotiating prices with Asda by means of a special 'contract range', and, most importantly, helped enable the overall profit margin to be gradually doubled from 16 per cent to 32 per cent during his term of office.

Another noteworthy incident that Tony remembers from this period was a surprise order from Marks and Spencer for one thousand dozen bedjackets. This supposedly arose from a conversation between the wives of the Chairmen of the two great undertakings (M&S and Courtaulds) at some event, when the question was asked: 'Why don't we sell your bedjackets in our stores?' This was not the usual method of M&S marketing, but illustrates the way that things often happen! Accordingly, Tony sourced the 12,000 bedjackets from a manufacturer in Leek and the deal was done.

Tony's assistant, Michael Base, was a very energetic contributor to the Underwear department's management team, and also played a major part in the development of Dukes and Morley scarves and gloves.

Staff Memories from the late 1980s and 90s

Amanda O'Leary started with Brettles in 1987, working for Bob Ash, who at the time was solely responsible for buying nightwear and lingerie, before being promoted to Merchandise Director, which involved overseeing the buying in all departments. Bob was highly experienced and respected in his field, and she gained a great wealth of knowledge from him on the buying side, although she already had years of experience in textile technology, design and fabric converting.

Amanda remembers that Bob was seen as quite a fearsome person, and was a slow starter in the mornings. 'He liked to come in and sit down with his pipe (smoking indoors was strictly forbidden), a cup of coffee (made by Amanda) and his paper. By 10am he would have had his second cuppa and was ready for work. Staff members would approach the office, cautiously peer round the door and wait for me to either beckon them in or discreetly signal for them to come back later.'

Amanda particularly remembers one occasion when Gary Spendlove returned to the office after a six-week trip to the Middle East. 'He came along to our department to proudly show Bob the orders which he had taken for nightwear and lingerie; they were considerable and not to be sneezed at. Gary had given away a little margin here and there to secure the orders, but Bob, having not been consulted first, was furious. He seized the orders, ripped them in half and threw them in the bin. Gary stormed out after making some comment that Bob was never grateful, or words to that effect. I had thought about taking cover under my desk, but decided to make Bob a calming cuppa instead. After puffing on his pipe and drinking his tea, Bob retrieved the orders from the bin, sellotaped them back together, then went to thank Gary for his efforts.' Perhaps lessons learned all round!

Amanda went from being 'the office girl' to Assistant Buyer, which enabled her to use more of her previous experience and knowledge in textiles. She started to accompany Bob on his buying trips to Istanbul (a place she has continued to visit for 25 years), Spain, and various parts of the UK.

Amanda's perception was that Bob's bark was worse than his bite, and this became apparent as the years went on and he began to mellow. He was winding down towards retirement, and with mutual respect their roles became reversed, to the point that he would come into the office in the morning, make Amanda's coffee, then after his morning ritual ask her what he could do to help!

Elaine Salmon joined Brettles in March 1987, just six weeks before the company was moved from Belper to Alfreton. She remembers that Hortons of Ripley were contracted to run a works bus from Belper to Alfreton, calling at Heage and Ripley, and this ran for over ten years. She saw how the move from the 'rabbit warren' of departments at Belper into 'open plan' at Alfreton brought about a shared sense of the big team, and that staff of different departments got to know each other better. The social side was strong. Elaine remembers the Christmas parties at the Palais and Ritz in Nottingham and the Pink Coconut in Derby, and one at Higham Farm in 1999. Other outings included cycling round Rutland Water, tenpin bowling and the toboggan run at Swadlincote.

Elaine worked in the Accounts department with Paul Naylor, with Peter Knight as Credit Controller. She remembers some quaint terms being used, such as 'Renders' meaning creditors to whom money was owed. Company computerisation only began with the move to Alfreton, the company using a bespoke package, also used by Coats Viyella. In those early days of computerisation, much of the work apart from initial data input was done externally by a computer bureau in Derby.

When Gary Spendlove became Sales Director in 1993, Elaine became his PA and was also involved in Export work, along with Toni Elliot and Elaine Boyman. Elaine had been PA to

John Simpson when she met her future husband Ernie Lovell on a course. Ernie was a senior Courtaulds Training Officer who worked at the Courtaulds Training Centre at Woodside in Warwickshire. Toni Elliot made a positive contribution to the company's expanding export business, and was climbing the ladder of the young promotables. Unfortunately she was tragically killed in a car accident; her funeral was attended by most employees, and she was sadly missed.

When Chilprufe took over in 1997, the new management moved Elaine into the main Sales office. Then, when Chris Ham replaced Gary as Sales Director later that year, she worked as his PA.

The former Hosiery dept, now Belper Orangery (MacDonalds).

The frontage of Brettles buildings today, from roundabout.
Both photographs courtesy of Ray Marjoram and Belper Historical Society Collection.

Sales Manager Visits to Ireland

Gary Spendlove was promoted to Sales Manager in 1989, which involved regular visits to many different areas. Here he recalls a trip that he always enjoyed making.

Part of the Sales Manager's function was to visit the area reps and area sales managers. The general strategy was to boost trade and develop direct management links with key retail accounts. One of my favourite visits was two or three days in Northern Ireland with our esteemed Irish agent Lawrence Reid. Laurie introduced me to many of the finest retailers and department stores in the province. On my visits I built a lasting picture of the deep divide between Republicans and Unionists, and between many Catholics and Protestants, although clearly a huge majority of people had a great desire for peace. Thanks to God that, with the hard work and determination of many politicians, church leaders and ordinary people, the peacemakers eventually won the day.

I always had a warm welcome from our retail friends, and the vivacious Maureen Pimbley of Anderson & McAuley was always a 'good call'. We were always delighted to 'scratch the pad' in Andy Macs. The warm humour of the staff of Wattersons of Omagh made this one of my favourite calls. The buyer Veda Short and her assistant Lillian always had a ready smile and wonderful wit. Sadly, Veda lost her life in the Omagh bomb massacre. The textile world and the world as a whole shared a very dark day at the sad loss of a wonderful lady.

It was always a pleasure to visit the Houstons stores. Mr Kennedy, with his sons Steven, John and Phillip were always the perfect Irish gentlemen. The courtesy of Paul Cuddy and his father in Magherafelt was also memorable. We always made time for a coffee, and it always felt like I was with friends. I also have good memories of Dunlop & Carson, Moores of Coleraine, the White House in Portrush, and Marshalls of Saintfield, and of finishing the day with Roberta at Menarys, which was always a pleasant way to end my visit.

A bracing walk with Laurie Reid on and around the Giant's Causeway stands out as a fond memory. The city walls of Londonderry are also very impressive and well worth a visit. The North of Ireland has so much potential for tourism; thank God the continuing peace in the twenty-first century allows many people to visit and enjoy the historic beauty of the province.

Following my two or three days in the north I would board the train for Dublin and go on to visit customers in the south. I always enjoyed this journey, usually via Dundalk and Drogheda, a chance to relax after the full days in the north with their early starts and late finishes, and an opportunity to grab an hour's sleep. Apart that is from one occasion when four rough-looking Irish lads took exception to my broad Derbyshire accent and proceeded to berate me for most of the Irish 'troubles' over the last three hundred years. In fairness, an amount of alcohol had been consumed but a very diplomatic guard and several transport police ensured my safe arrival in the capital of the Irish Republic.

Dublin – what an amazing city! But I have never known a place so unimpressed by celebrity. At different times I saw Damon Hill, Bob Geldof, Bono and other members of U2 as well as one or two boy band members, but not one of them was hounded by the paparazzi or even autograph hunters.

Our Brettles agents for the Irish Republic were a highly regarded father and son duo, Stan and Randal Ferguson. The company previously had a very popular agent in Mr Hilary Shanahan. Hilary's wife was the Buyer from the Roches Stores group. He had held company performance records for sales of nightwear and dressing gowns. When the Roches orders were hand-picked in the Lingerie department you would see quite a mountain of quality individually boxed items for this major export customer.

Stan and Randal had a difficult act to follow, but they were very successful with the high-class Dublin department stores, especially Clerys, whose Buyer Pat Hussey and her staff were strong supporters of the Brettles brand, and always an absolute pleasure to deal with.

On one of my earlier visits to Dublin, accommodation had been arranged for me at the renowned Burlington Hotel. Due to a 'faux pas' in the booking arrangement there were a number of problems with the hotel, resulting in a stern letter from Stan Ferguson to the hotel manager suggesting that the hotel 'make amends'. As a result of Stan's letter I was personally invited to return to the Burlington Hotel and offered VIP treatment. I was given their top suite for the duration of my visit, complete with separate bedrooms and circular jacuzzi bath, which incidentally you had to walk up some steps to; I was certainly given the 'royal treatment'. In fact I was told that Henry Kissinger had been a previous occupant of that suite, along with a number of celebrities. Sadly, though, this accommodation was somewhat out of my price range on subsequent visits! But it was a most acceptable experience on that occasion.

Travels Abroad

Being Sales Manager and later Sales Director involved considerable overseas travel. Coming from a mining family (my father and great grandfather both worked at the local Denby Drury Lowe Colliery) was no preparation for many years of international travel. My first ever flight in an aircraft was a holiday to Italy, aged twenty. A few years later I clearly recollect, on a morning flight between Jeddah and Riyadh, being the only passenger in the first-class cabin of a Saudia 747. My thoughts still went back to family holidays in a caravan in Skegness or a cosy guest house in Scarborough. How I loved those family times – but how life had changed.

Left: As the local mines closed, many Derbyshire miners entered the textile industry. Here is a scene from Denby Drury Lowe Colliery.

I had no inclination when I started in 1973 that the Brettles path would allow me to visit almost one hundred countries. It included exciting visits to China, walking on the Great Wall, visiting Tiananmen Square and the 'Forbidden City' and also meeting many native Chinese people who kindly permitted me to partake of their hospitality – although I declined second helpings on most occasions. Snake, scorpion and cat are delicacies from the Far East that I would refuse in future. A whole sheep's brain on a wet night in the Lebanon's Bekaa Valley was hard to consume, but a Lebanese mezza is quite delicious, especially when washed down with the local Arak.

My Middle East trips have many memories. On one of numerous visits to the island of Bahrain, I was delighted to note we had twelve customers in and around the capital of Manama. But I was also pleasantly surprised to call in at a local garage and see Silkolene oil and Swarfega for sale. So not only were Belper companies selling thermal underwear to the Arab states, we were also selling oil back to the Middle East!

More negatively, I have been invited to public executions, but have always declined as I consider them to be barbaric. It still shocks me that this method of retribution is practised in many countries.

A first-hand experience of conflict, in Lebanon and Kuwait, was quite traumatic, in particular as I met so many lovely people in these places. The Kuwait Sheraton was a favourite hotel with a great restaurant. The Marriott Hotel, which had been an ocean liner, was a great location for a game of tennis with my good friend Bev Cruickshank. It was a sad experience just after the Iraq invasion to see these beautiful hotels largely destroyed. I personally had a very close call after leaving the Intercontinental Hotel in Amman in Jordan. After checking out and flying directly back to the UK, I arrived home in Belper about 12 hours later to learn from national TV that the same hotel had been wrecked by a massive car bomb.

Along with the amazing architecture of our old European cities, I have been fortunate to visit many ancient places. Pompeii, Rome, Ephesus and Cairo hold many memories, although Petra in Jordan would be my favourite. Before I lapse into a travellers' guide, it is enough to say that joining the company in 1973 allowed a local boy a wide world of opportunity which continues to the present day.

10. BRETTLES WITH SLENDERELLA

Gary Spendlove was one of the six managers who had earlier made a bid to buy the company from the parent business, Courtaulds Textiles, in 1996. Unfortunately for the buyout team, the Courtaulds main board decided to accept a bid from a major Leicester underwear producer, Chilprufe Ltd. Although the takeover had potentially created a major European textile business, the new company was destined not to succeed but to enter administration early in the new millennium. Meanwhile Gary agreed a redundancy deal with Chilprufe in October 1997 which included the purchase of the Belper factory shop, from which base he soon saw other possibilities for the future.

The Slenderella Story

As a young sales rep in Scotland in the 1970s, Gary had also become very aware of the Slenderella nightware and lingerie collections. The brand enjoyed a wide distribution and was sold in many of Scotland's top stores, including Jenners of Edinburgh, R.W. Forsyth, Frasers, Alexander Wilkies, Turnbull and Wilson, Arnotts and Patrick Thompsons to name but a few. The Scottish agent for Slenderella was the highly regarded Ian Lindsay. The brand was then produced by S. Newman Ltd., mainly on Tyneside. It was considered that the company manufactured a prized dressing gown collection. The quilted items were luxurious and aimed at the middle- to high-class market sector. Slenderella enjoyed an excellent reputation, producing exclusive styles both for the company's own label and for contract markets, including major department stores.

From humble home-spun beginnings in the East End of London in the 1920s, Slenderella had grown to acquire its own factory. This was destroyed by bombs in 1942, and they moved to Middlesex. Two years later, as the demands of the Second World War increased, the factory was requisitioned by the Ministry of Aircraft Production. The decision was then made to move to a large production unit in South Shields. From there, Slenderella became a recognised national brand.

The complete Slenderella story is told in Andrew Miller's book *The Earl of Petticoat Lane*.[1] As with Brettles, there are fascinating connections to the Royal Family and other renowned celebrities. Hollywood legends Elizabeth Taylor and Hedy Lamarr were known to have worn the company's products. The company were delighted when Miss Taylor and the cast of the acclaimed film *Little Women* publicised their garments. Further international acclaim followed when the company helped create Miss Lamarr's wardrobe exclusively for the golden screen classic *Samson and Delilah*.

In 1997 Gary discovered that the Slenderella brand was available for acquisition, with an almost limitless potential for development. He held discussions with Michael Freedman, as Director of S. Newman Ltd. and owner of the brand, which were successful. The legalities for the purchase of the Slenderella brand were undertaken by Robinsons solicitors of Derby, and the new company, Slenderella Wholesale Ltd, was incorporated on 19th November 1997. The owners are recorded as Gary with his wife Gaynor as the Company Secretary. The first wholesale premises were a small room at the rear of the Belper retail shop on Chapel Street, on which Gary had taken the lease.

The first retail customer to place an order from the new firm was Edna Dale of Leek, and the first multiple order was placed by the Beatties group of Wolverhampton. In the first year of trading, the company received the *Lingerie Buyer* magazine award for the UK's best classic nightwear collection, sponsored by Dupont. For the next two years the brand achieved the runners–up trophy, but again won the coveted crystal pyramid in 2001. The company has also received industry and Chamber of Commerce awards.

From Chilprufe to Slenderella

Chilprufe had taken over the Brettles business and the associated brands at the end of 1996. All of the other historic brands created a very strong ladieswear offer for the new company. However, it is worth noting that at a 1997 sales meeting in Alfreton the Chilprufe sales team believed the new Slenderella company to be a strong competitor.

No records are available to state the reason for the final demise of Chilprufe, but poor cash flow, declining quality and a consequent downturn in demand were certainly contributing factors. Chilprufe was put into receivership early in 2002. This allowed a sale agreement for the Brettles brand to be achieved between Stuart David Maddison for Chilprufe Ltd (in receivership) and Slenderella Wholesale Ltd. The Slenderella management paid a modest five-figure sum for the brand rights of Brettles. As part of the same deal, the Walker Reid brand was also acquired. Both brands were assigned to Slenderella by the Patents Office on 12th June 2002, and this greatly strengthened the offer available from the young Belper company. The agreement included the purchase of a large quantity of finished merchandise. Gary Spendlove recalls the event as 'the best day's business I ever did'.

Thus was the Brettle brand rescued and brought it back to its historic home town of Belper.

Growth and Celebration

Meanwhile the Slenderella office and retail outlet had moved from Chapel Street to the old Co-op building on King Street, Belper. This new address allowed warehouse space for twelve thousand items of stock. However, the rapid growth of the company necessitated a further move, this time to the former premises of another historic Belper business, Flanders Ltd, owned by the Litchfield family. Sadly the move meant the closure of the retail shop for a time, leaving many long-standing customers disappointed.

At first, from July 2002, the company just leased and occupied the former Flanders warehouse in Queen Street, and created some office space there. Again, due to swift expansion and the need to store a large dressing gown collection, an approach was made to John and Roger Litchfield, acting for Coppice Property, to purchase the whole of the site. The amicable negotiations were completed, and the company again had the capacity to expand. By 2003, it was supplying over 700 customers in the UK.

The year 2003 was the recognised 200-year anniversary of the establishment of Brettles in Belper, and time for a major celebration. Over 300 friends, guests and former employees attended the event, and many artefacts and historic memorabilia were displayed at various venues in the town. A 'Miss Slenderella' competition was won by local girl Frankie Corbett. For the event a booklet containing the condensed history of Brettles was created. So an anniversary that could easily have never happened was celebrated in style.

Above: Some retired employees at bicentennial celebrations, 2003.

Left: 2003 Bicentennial Cake with Peter & Mary Oakley, Dena Bell & Joy Exton.

Geoff Melbourne with Brettles original oil painting, 2003.

Former Management and Staff on Chapel Street during the Brettles Reunion in 2003.

Group of past and present employees outside Brettles former export officel, 2003.

Left: Group of Employees at sponsored cricket match, Belper Sportsground, 2003.

Below: Gary receiving award, 2003 (by kind Permission of JMS Photography).

In 2007 the warehouse was purchased, along with the adjacent office block. This was a big financial commitment, for an expanding and ambitious company. The staff joined in with contractors to get the building into shape, with renovations and redecoration needed. Its opening coincided with Gary's fiftieth birthday, and the staff laid on a party in the new offices, with Blues Brothers music. There was a great sense of achievement and celebration.

The next big step forward was in May 2008, when by popular demand the new Brettles Retail Shop was opened in Days Lane at the side of the premises, run by Julie Wheelhouse, with customers travelling considerable distances to make their purchases.

Above: Miss Slenderella Frankie Corbett driving past Slenderella's second home, 2004.

Left: Local MP Patrick McLoughlin and Slenderella staff.

Below: GS and Amanda O'Leary with BBC newsreader Kate Adie.

Above: GS and open-air Snooker, Beijing, China. 2006.

Right: Shanghai Skyline from hotel, China. December 2008.

Below: GS and Amanda at Korean meal, Quindhao, China. December 2008.

Right: Ablutions outside Sultan Hammet Great Mosque, Istanbul, May 2009.

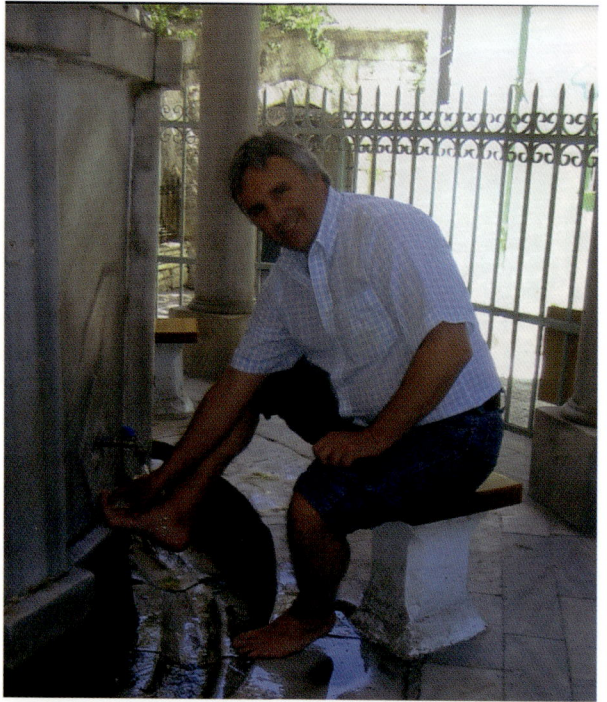

Below: Harvindar Singh Sodhi, GS and Amanda at the Taj Mahal, India, May 2010.

Left: Captaining the Chinese Olympic Yacht, Qingdhao Bay, China.

At the time of writing, all the Brettles product groups are continuing to grow and garments are purchased daily in many retail shops in the British Isles. Export growth continues, with overseas sales contributing more than 12 per cent of the annual turnover. The quality and value offered will ensure the brand trades successfully into the twenty-first century. The history is wonderful and the future is very exciting.

A Winning Team

The current Brettles-Slenderella team includes a number who worked for the old Brettles company.

Geoffrey Futter was the earliest of the present team to join the old company, in 1965, as described in Chapter 9. After an absence of 38 years, he joined the present company in February 2010. He recalls that on 'his first day back' he was helping to man a stand at the MODA exhibition at the NEC. Since then he has been employed in a very versatile way on a range of work, according to what is needed at the time.

Pat Thawley has spent the longest of all the team with Brettles. She joined the old company in 1968, working in the 'Entering Room' then in the Lingerie department and also in the warehouse.

Sue Brindley joined Brettles in 1972 and worked in the internal Post Office, in the Entering Room and in the factory shop. In 1997, when the present company took over the Belper shop, Gary invited Sue to stay there, which she did. In 2007 Pat also started, and they became joint warehouse managers.

Elaine Salmon joined Brettles in March 1987, just six weeks before the company moved to Alfreton. She worked in the Accounts department, then became Gary's PA when he was Sales Director from 1993. In January 2000 Elaine and others were moved to the Chilprufe headquarters in Leicester. As Elaine lived in Ripley, the long commute to Leicester was inconvenient, and she was glad of the chance to leave in November 2000 to rejoin colleagues at Slenderella as Accounts Administrator. As such she was also involved in data input, though the company then only had two PCs, both in the warehouse office. Elaine has worked on credit control, chasing debtors and making sales calls.

Amanda O'Leary also started with Brettles in 1987, having already had some years of textiles experience. She became an Assistant Merchandiser at Brettles, and is now a Manager at Slenderella, a role in which she travels abroad extensively.

One recent member (who actually retired at the end of 2010) was **Margaret Dunstan**, who worked for Chilprufe and their original parent company Coats Viyella from 1987, in the Sales office at Leicester. From 1997 she was based partly at Leicester and partly at Brettles Sales office at Alfreton, staying with Chilprufe until the end then working briefly for the Receivers. Margaret started with Slenderella on 27th January 2003 as Sales Office Administrator. She brought many contacts and opened new doors for the new company. After a year she was promoted to Sales Office Manager.

The team also includes some who were not part of the old Brettles but worked for other textile companies, including **Julie Horne**, who was a Quality Controller for Jaeger Knitwear. She joined Slenderella in 2003 as Merchandise Assistant with Amanda and doubles up as Health & Safety Officer. Julie's position involves marketing, photography and assisting the general manager in producing new collections, including various international visits. In the UK, she is also involved with mail order customers, produces photographic images for promotional material and liaises with a modelling agency.

On a very positive note, we have recently welcomed Michael Meredith back to the company after many years of working with different brands in the ladieswear business. Mike brings to the company a wealth of sales and marketing experience.

The Late Noughties

All the staff I spoke to perceive the 'late noughties' as years of overall growth, especially the period from 2008, even as other companies have languished. The company has 'kept its finger on the pulse' of supply and demand changes. On the supply side, it has changed its focus from UK and European to Far East sourcing, due to the dwindling of the UK supply chain, whilst Italy and Turkey, both previously big suppliers, were becoming more expensive. Two new Brettles ranges have been introduced in the past four years – 'Gaspé', a range of 'young and sexy' lingerie and microfibre underwear which is ideal for the smaller lingerie shops (in contrast to that supplied by Walker Reid for the large multiples); and 'Slenders' briefs, which compete well on price with Kayser slips. The company has a stable comprehensive lingerie catalogue of products that sell well from year to year, whilst nightwear and swimwear brochures are changed each season in line with fashions.

Up & Coming Model Hannah with International Model Caprice.

Right: Slenderella model with brands (Slenders, Brettles, Walker Reid, Vedonis) in the *Lingerie Buyer,* February 2006.

Far Right: Front cover of Slenderella promotional leaflet. 2008?

Slenderella®
Beautiful Lingerie & Nightwear

Vedonis®
Next to myself like....

Brands of Distinction

Slenderella®
Beautiful Lingerie & Nightwear

Brettles®
Since 1786

Slenders®
Double Comfort Briefs

Walker Reid®
Classic Quality

Stand M5

SLENDERELLA
L I N G E R I E

Classic Nightwear & Lingerie

Un pizzico di insolenza per Slenderella

Slenderella, marchio leader in Gran Bretagna per il segmento lingerie da notte, propone per questa stagione un look completamente rinnovato con una linea bis giovane e fresca: Sassy Slenderella. Il disegno, un gatto nero che porta un collier d'argento, compare su un'ampia gamma di capi come pantaloni

Slenderella model with the companies first european magazine article 2001.

Best Business Award with newsreader Peter Sissons and Rolls Royce Chairman Sir Ralph Robins.

Town Criers, Mr and Mrs Arthur Bellaby, announcing the return of Brettles to Belper.

Former Management; Peter Knight, Paul Crosby, George Morley, Doug Penton, Peter Sinnock, Gwyn Stevenson with Gary Spendlove during a tour of Belper North Mill.

The Chapel Street factory shop, 1998.

Ward of Cripplegate Within.

The Inhabitants of the Ward of Cripplegate Within offer their sincere congratulations to their Alderman, Harry Edward Augustus Twyford, on his election to the ancient and honourable office of Sheriff of the City of London and trust that he may be blessed with health and strength to carry out his important duties.

They feel confident that he will at all times fulfil those duties with honour to himself and to the satisfaction of his fellow citizens and that his Shrievalty will add lustre to the great reputation of that high office.

It is the earnest wish of the inhabitants of the Ward that he may be spared to continue for many years the good work he has performed for the Corporation of the City of London as Alderman of the Ward.

Dated the 9th day of November 1934.

Hugh G. Taylor. Deputy Alderman.

G. Mart.   G. E. Wood.
F. G. Wigley.   H. C. Barry.
W. Nicholson.   G. J. Selby.

} Members of the Court of Common Council for the Ward of Cripplegate Within.

A. Hanley   Frank   Ward Clerk

Cripplegate Complimentary letter to Harry Twyford, Sherrif of London, 1934 (Photographer Nick Locket).

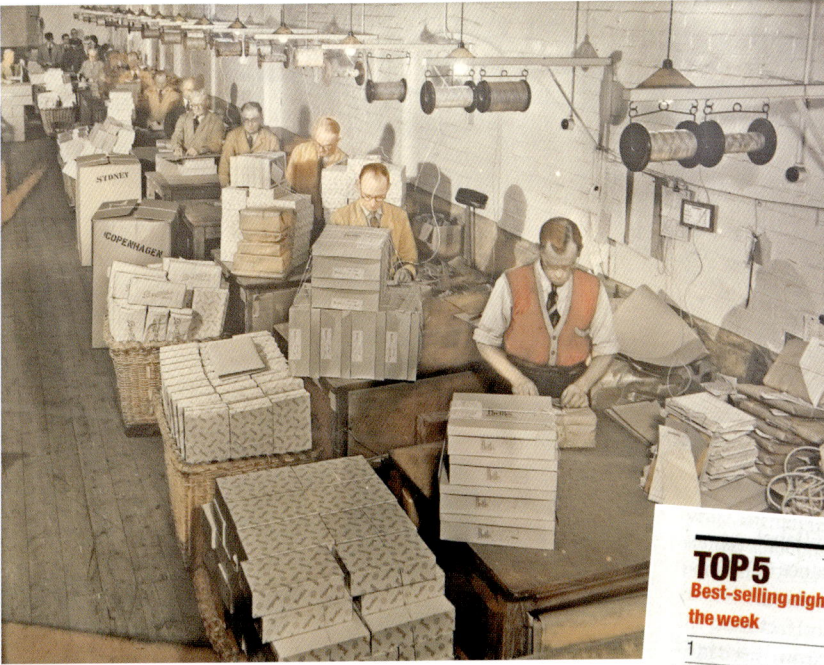

Packing department 1960s.

Right: This cutting from last Octobers 'Drapers' confirms Slenderella's position in the market. (Reproduced by kind permission 'Drapers').

TOP 5
Best-selling nightwear brands of the week

1	Slenderella
2	Marjolaine
3	Pill
4	Hanro
5	Triumph

Drapers spoke to 50 independents about their women's lingeri

10 Drapers October 1 2010

Slenderella factory, Queen Street, Belper.

GS with Miss England.

Gary's Final Thoughts

I have alluded to the wonderful stories and achievements of so many Brettles staff I have known. So, around the time of the Brettles 200-year celebration, I decided that this splendid history should be recorded. The highs and lows of a progressive company are apparent through the chapters.

The story nearly ended in 1997, when after the Chilprufe takeover it was considered that the Brettles brand would cease to actively trade. I recall that, after taking my redundancy from Chilprufe and launching the Slenderella brand, a personal ambition was to bring the Brettles name back to Belper and re-establish it as a private company. This was achieved in 2003 after the Leicester business entered administration. We immediately developed a high-quality pure cotton underwear collection, quickly followed by a seamfree thermal range. Both of these groups of products enjoy a wide UK and export distribution. Add to this dressing gowns, pure cotton nightwear with lingerie, and the historic brand grows into the twenty-first century.

Interestingly, apart from consumer and historic interest, we have had offers to purchase the brand, one a substantial bid from a mail order catalogue. Naturally the 'not for sale' sign was shown. After all, many of us consider the custodianship of the brand to be priceless. The garments are also sold more extensively via the internet.

My recorded memories in this and the previous chapter are but a few recollections of one individual, which would not have happened without that first step through the Brettles revolving door. Thousands of people have enjoyed their time at the company over the years. To many it was much more than a way to pay the mortgage; in fact a lot of employees met their future spouses while working there. This book has given but a brief overview of a historic company and of its 'phoenix' that trades successfully today. As 'Custodians of the Brand' I know that all of my staff will work hard to ensure a healthy future. My thanks to them for their dedicated support.

Acknowledgement

Many thanks to Rod Hawgood, without whose diligent research, this book would not have been written. Also many thanks to Nick Lockett for his photographic professionalism.

Obituary

Sadly, just before the book was published we lost two former senior members of staff. Ernie Lovell, who made so many positive contributions to the sales side of the company. Also, former Managing Director, Tony Gray who was delighted to add his wide knowledge of the textile trade to the contents.

Both I'm sure would, have enjoyed reading the history of "Brettles in Belper".

11. CONFERENCE PHOTOGRAPHS

Glyn Bailey and Sandy Taylor(facing away from camera) Ian Lindsay was a key salesman for Slenderella in the 1970s,and also a major player in the Brettles sales force.

Roger Knowles organised the company cars, and operated the internal computer systems.

Sales office manageress Mary Bailey, warehouse Director Graham Newton. Credit control manager Peter Knight ensured the company maintained excellent cash flow.

Mike Base, Bob Ash(partly obscured) and Glyn Bailey.

Key accounts executive, Don Mcleish.

Tony Gray and the great organiser Elaine Lovell.

Jimmy Lewis added his wit and sophistication to several sales conferences.

Charles Powell, was greatly respected in the hosiery industry, and played a major role in the success of the factory.

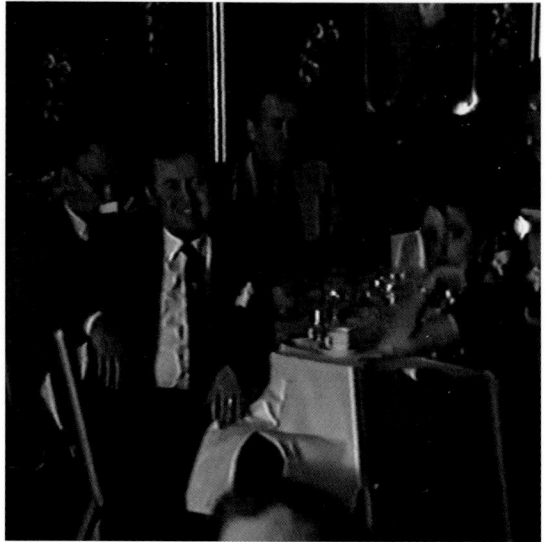

Personel manager George Morley. Experienced sales force members Stewart Perrin and Fred Blakey.

Michelle Hobson and her team of professional models add glamour to one of the Belfry sales conferences.

Miss United Kingdom Michelle Hobson.

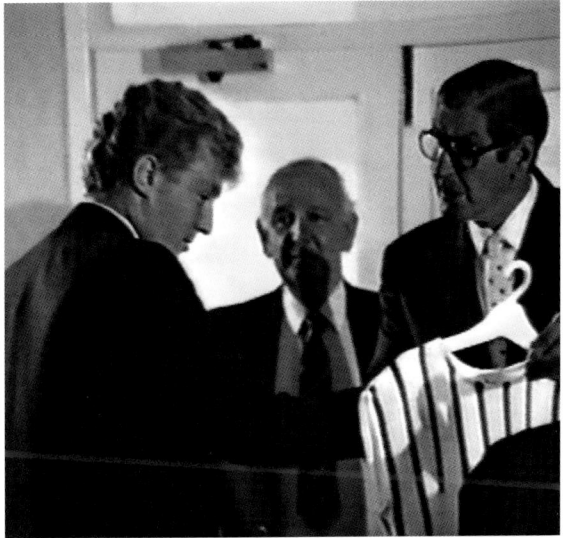

Above: Popular Irishmen in the sales force, Randal Ferguson and Laurie Reid discuss the 1986 knitwear collection with retail expert Bob Hoadley.

Stan Ferguson, the agent for Eire.

Above: East Anglian area manager Terry Purkiss was often asked to mentor the young trainee sales people.

Conferences were very important, twice yearly, in the company calendar, usually attended by over sixty of the company sales team and management. These black and white photographs are "stills" taken from VHS videos filmed in the 1980's. The quality is therefore somewhat lacking in definition but an important part of the story never the less.

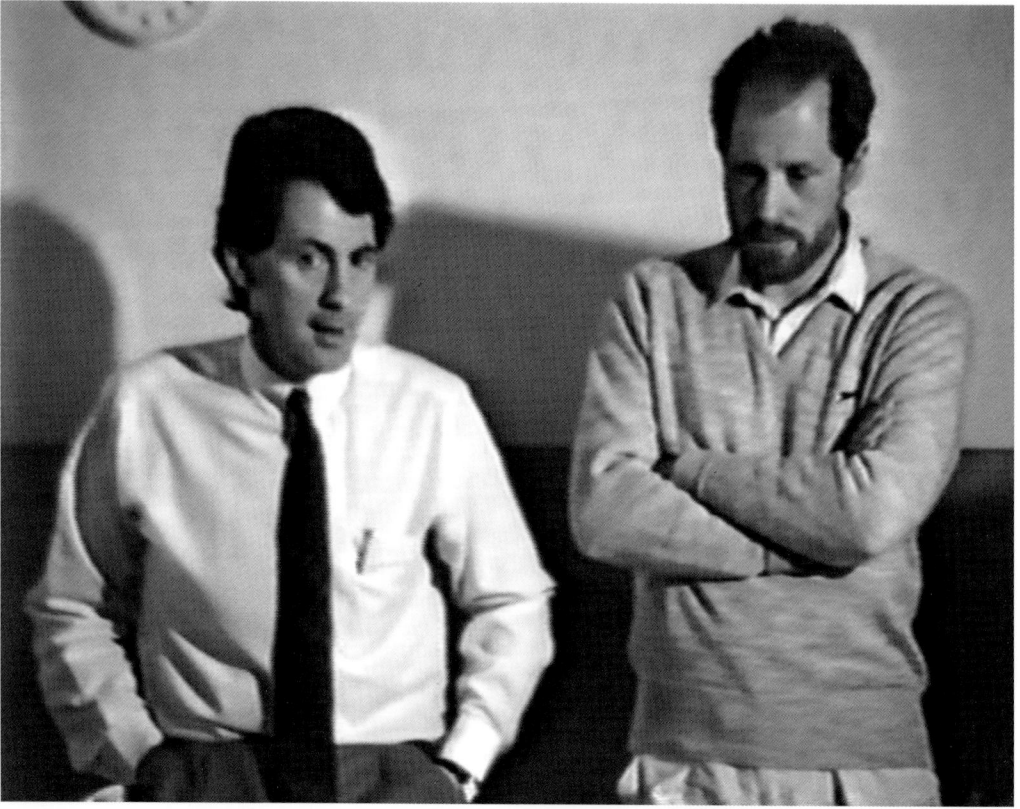

Thoughtful questions from Mike Meredith and Graham Edwards.

Left: Ken Royle and Ken Mortimer considering the latest lingerie styles.

Right: Sales rep George Tunnicliffe was always guaranteed a captive audience when giving a presentation.

Twice salesman of the year Gordan Bayley.

The ever popular Glyn Bailey.

Sarah Emery worked tirelessly to implement new computer systems and expand the company's marketing profile.

REFERENCES

Chapter 1

1 Figures from pages 15–18, 1845 Report and 'Some Particulars of the Past' from *A History of the Machine-Wrought Hosiery and Lace Manufactures* by William Felkin, London: Longmans, Green, and Co., 1867.

2 Pages 164–165, *The Civil, Political and Mechanical History of the Framework Knitters in Europe and America* by Gravenor Henson, Nottingham: printed by Richard Sutton, 1831.

3 Page 299, 'A New Historical and Descriptive View of Derbyshire' by D.P. Davies (Belper 1811).

4 Ch 3–4, *The Strutts and the Arkwrights 1758–1830* by R.S. Fitton & A.P. Wadsworth, Manchester: Manchester University Press, 1958.

5 'William Strutt's Fire-proof and Iron-framed Buildings 1792–1812' by H.R. Johnson & A.W. Kempton.

6 Page11, *A History of George Brettle & Co. Ltd 1801–1964* by Negley Harte, published by the author, 1973.

7 'Ince's Pedigrees' f.212 and Strutt MSS, Derby Public Library.

8 Page 67, Fitton & Wadsworth, op. cit.

9 'Chevening: One of Derbyshire's Lost Arts' by Marjorie Blount, in *Derbyshire Life* Volume 17, January – March 1948.

10 Duffield Parish Church Marriage Register, 16th April 1759 ; Ince's Pedigrees ff.212 &223.

11 Page 13, Negley Harte op. cit.

12 Manchester Central Library: Strutt MSS, Belper Ledger 1792–1803, f.194.

13 Strutt MSS, Belper Ledger 1792–1803, f 194.

14 Confirmed by Kent's Directory for 1803 and for 1804.

15 Pages 15–16, Negley Harte, op. cit.

16 Brief Account of Ward Brettle & Ward by William Ward and John Finney, 1823.

17 Ibid.

18 Ibid.

Chapter 2

1 Brief Account of Ward Brettle & Ward by William Ward and John Finney, 1823.

2 Ibid.

3 Page 20, *A History of George Brettle & Co. Ltd. 1801–1964* by Negley Harte, published by the author, 1973.

4 Pages 263 & 275, 1845 Report to Parliamentary Commission, Appendix 2.

5 *Derby Evening Telegraph* article on 'George Brettle & Co. Ltd.' on 5th March 1954.

6 Ibid.

7 Page 47, *Yarns*, Volume 1, No.2, April 1929.

8 Page 25, Negley Harte, op. cit.

9 Page 32, ibid.

10 Brief Account of Ward Brettle & Ward by William Ward and John Finney, 1823.

11 Page 20, Negley Harte, op. cit.

12 Page 100 & 242, *History, Gazetteer & Directory of the County of Derby* by Stephen Glover, 1829.

13 From *Buildings of England: London* by Nikolaus Pevsner, Harmondsworth: Penguin, 1952.

14 Page 283, *Gentleman's Magazine* NS, clll, ii (1833), and *Derby Mercury* 11th September 1833.

15 Page 53, Negley Harte, op. cit.

16 Page 20, ibid.

17 Pages 76–77, ibid.

18 Probate 11/1856. & Page 58, Negley Harte, op. cit.

19 Page 62, Negley Harte, op. cit.

Chapter 3

1 Page 62, *A History of George Brettle & Co. Ltd. 1801–1964* by Negley Harte, published by the author, 1973.

2 *History, Gazetteer & Directory of the County of Derby* by Stephen Glover, Derby, 1829, quoted in 'Framework Knitting & Hosiery', web article by Mary Smedley.

3 Page 275, 1845 Report to Parliamentary Commission, Appendix 2.

4 Page 85, ibid.

5 Page 226, ibid.

6 Page 88, ibid, John Rogers quote

7 Page 238, 1841 Report from Select Committee on the Exportation of Machinery, Appendix 3

8 Page 85 of 1845 Report and page 382 of 1854–55 Report.

9 Page 275, 1845 Report.

10 Page 236, ibid.

11 Page 82, ibid.

12 Page 305, 'English Reports', Chancery XXVI.

13 Page 342, VCH. Surrey 3, 1911.

14 Article in *Derby Mercury*, 29th May 1867.

15 Page 276, 1845 Report, Appendix 2.

16 Page 279, ibid.

17 Page 70, Negley Harte, op. cit.

18 Ibid & ref 15.

19 Page 277, 1855 Report.

20 Page 263, 1845 Report.

21 Page 269, ibid.

22 Page 76, Negley Harte, op. cit.

23 Page 247, 1855 Report, Appendix 2.

24 Page 725, *Gardners History, Gazetteer of the County of Oxford* (Peterborough, 1852) and page 140, *Kelly's Directory of Oxfordshire* (London, 1899).

25 Page 78, Negley Harte, op. cit.

26 Page 248, 1845 Report.

27 Page 262, ibid.

28 Pages 21–24, *A.J. Mundella, 1825–1897: the Liberal background to the Labour movement* by W.H.G. Armytage, London: Benn, 1951.

29 Page 291, *History and Gazatteer of Derbyshire* by Samuel Bagshaw, Sheffield, 1846.

30 Page 562, 1845 Report, evidence of Thomas Whittaker McCallum.

31 Page 138, *Yarns* Volume 2, 1930.

32 Page 83, Negley Harte, op. cit.

33 *Derby Evening Telegraph* article, 5th March 1954.

34 Patent 918, 1870.

35 Page 85, Negley Harte, op. cit.

36 Page 60, *Derbyshire* by Nikolas Pevsner, Harmondsworth: Penguin, 1953.

37 Page 75, *I. & R. Morley: A Record of a Hundred Years* by Frederick M. Thomas, London: Chiswick Press, 1900.

Chapter 4

1 Will of George Henry Brettle, Principal Probate Registry, Somerset House.

2 *Kelly's Handbook to the Titled, Landed and Official Classes* for 1888 and for 1901.

3 Page 2124, *Kelly's Directory of Kent, Surrey and Sussex, London 1887*.

4 Page 88, *A History of George Brettle & Co. Ltd. 1801–1964* by Negley Harte, published by the author, 1973.

5 Pages 147–151, *The British Hosiery & Knitwear Industry: its History and Organisation* by F.A. Wells, Newton Abbot: David & Charles, 1972.

6 Page 89, Negley Harte, op.cit.

7 Will of Helen Twyford, Principal Probate Registry, Somerset House.

8 Page 140, *Dod's Parliamentary Companion for 1880*, 2nd edition, London, 1880.

9 1882 Partnership Agreement, quoted on page 93, Negley Harte, op. cit.

10 Page 13, *Yarns* Volume 3, No. 1, 1931.

11 Page 23, *Yarns* Volume 1, No. 1, 1929.

12 Page 99, Negley Harte, op. cit.

13 Letter written by 'Thomas Paul', reproduced June 1914.

14 Page 62 *Yarns* Volume 1, No.2 (1929) and *Derby Evening Telegraph*, 5th March 1954.

15 *Derby Mercury*, 11th April 1913.

Chapter 5

1 Will of H.R. Twyford, proved 13th May 1913, Public Probate Records, Somerset House.

2 Page106, *A History of George Brettle & Co. Ltd. 1801–1964* by Negley Harte, published by the author, 1973.

3 *Derbyshire Advertiser*, 16th January 1959.

4 Page 134, Negley Harte, op. cit.

5 'Framework Knitting and Hosiery', web article by historian Mary Smedley.

6 Page 170, *The British Hosiery & Knitwear Industry: its History and Organisation* by F.A. Wells, Newton Abbot: David & Charles, 1972; and Import Duties Act Inquiry data in 'The Hosiery Industry' in *Studies in Industrial Organization,* ed. H.A. Silverman, London: Methuen, 1946 (reprinted London: Routledge, 2003).

7 Pages 119–20, Negley Harte, op. cit.

8 Pages 7–9, *Yarns,*Volume 1, No.1, 1929.

9 *Financial Times*, 18th April 1930.

10 *Yarns*, Volume 4, No. 2, 1932: Chairman's letter following Editorial.

11 George Brettle & Co. Profit & Loss Accounts 1928–1940, Derbyshire Records Office.

12 Mary Smedley, op. cit.

13 *The Banker*, May 1929.

14 *Drapers Record*, 3rd May 1930.

15 *The Times*, 27th August 1936.

16 Page 134, Negley Harte, op. cit.

17 'Contact' newsletters, nos. 1 & 2.

Chapter 6

1 Pages 75–86, 'Board of Trade Working Party Reports: Hosiery', 1940.

2 Page 147, *A History of George Brettle & Co. Ltd. 1801–1964* by Negley Harte, published by the author, 1973.

3 'Personality Parade – George Brettle & Co. Ltd., Belper', *Womens Wear News* 1951.

4 Brettles Employees Handbook.

5 Memoirs of Mr Syd Clarke, Accountant.

6 *Derbyshire Advertiser*, 16th January 1959.

7 Pages 148–50, Negley Harte, op.cit and company accounts.

8 'Flimsy Girl', poem by Sally Goldsmith in 'Threads' collection.

9 Pages 148–150, Negley Harte, op. cit. and company accounts.

Chapter 7

1 'George Brettle of Belper', article in *Hosiery Times*, March 1967.

2 Visit to Arabian Gulf and Saudi Arabia, Report 17th November 1975. T. Hollingworth, L. Collins & W. Thorpe

3 Visit to Arabian Gulf and Saudi Arabia, Report 24th March 1976. T. Hollingworth, L.H. Collins & W.O. Thorpe.

4 Visit to Saudi Arabia, Yemen and Libya, Report October 1976. N.A. Henderson & W.O. Thorpe.

5 Minutes of Export Meeting at Courtaulds Distributors, Birmingham, 19th May 1980.

6 Page 37, '*Body Style*, Issue no. 6, November 1987.

7 *Belper News*, 'Brettles Supplement', 1986.

Chapter 8

1 Page 99, *A History of George Brettle & Co. Ltd. 1801–1964* by Negley Harte, published by the author, 1973.

2 Page 20, *Yarns*, Volume 1, No. 1, 1929.

3 Pages 34 & 44, *Yarns*, Volume 1, No. 2, April 1929.

4 Page 33, *Yarns*, Volume 2, No. 1, January 1930.

5 Page 46, *Yarns*, Volume 3, No. 2, June 1931.

6 Page 48, *Yarns*, Volume 4, No. 2, December 1932.

7 Annual General Meeting minutes, 1938.

8 Page 141, *Yarns*, Volume 2, No. 4, October 1930.

9 Page 102, *Yarns*, Volume 3, No. 3, October 1931.

10 Page 48, *Yarns*, Volume 4, No. 2, December 1932.

11 Annual General Meeting minutes, 1937.

12 Annual General Meeting minutes, 1938.

13 Ibid.

14 Ibid.

15 Oberon Annual Accounts, 1941.

16 'Contact' newsletter, No. 2, December 1944.

17 Annual General Meeting minutes, 1944.

18 *Derbyshire Advertiser*, 16th January 1959.

19 Constitution and Rules of Oberon Sports and Social Club, 1964 edition.

20 Annual General Meeting minutes, 1969.

Chapter 10

1 Andrew Miller, *The Earl of Petticoat Lane: From an East End Chronicle to a West End Life*, London: Heinemann, 2006.

APPENDIX 1

Partners and Directors

1762–1800 Ward & Son
John Ward sr. 1762–1800
John Ward jr. 1790–1800

1801–1803 Ward Sharp & Co.
John Ward jr. 1801–1803
James Carter Sharp 1801–1803

1803–1834 Ward Brettle & Ward
John Ward 1803–1823
William Ward 1803–1833
George Brettle 1803–1834

1834–1930 Ward Sturt & Sharp
John Ward jr. 1834–?
Benjamin Ward 1834–?
James Carter Sharp 1834–?
? Sturt 1834–? (a rival concern)

1834–1914 George Brettle & Co.
George Brettle 1834–1835
Benjamin Hardwick 1835–1843 (trustee)
Alfred Brettle 1843–1856
Edward Brettle 1843–1867
George Henry Brettle 1843–1872
Thomas Wilson Elstob 1844–1866
William Smithyman Bean 1867–1876
Parmenas Martin Burgess 1867–1879
George Dickson 1867–1882
Frederick William Sharp 1867–1876
Mrs Helen Brettle-Twyford 1872–1882
Isaac Hanson 1880–1901
John Scott 1880–1903
Henry Robert Twyford 1882–1913
John Henry Mallard 1883–1904

1914–1963 George Brettle & Co. Ltd
Lionel Thomas Campbell Twyford 1914–1920 (Chairman)
Harry Edward Augustus Twyford 1914–1964 (MD 1914–1960, Chairman 1920–1963)
Alfred Murrell Gibson 1915–1941 ; part-time 1941–1949
Frank John Rayson 1920–1933 (Company Secretary 1914–1933)

Harry Richard Twyford 1925–1954 (Joint MD 1945–54, Deputy Chairman 1951–54)

Alfred Page 1937–1941

Ernest Edward Hall 1941–1946

Henry Osmont Randall 1938–1959 (Secretary 1934–1959)

Wallace Hoole Inch 1946–1959

Ernest Henry Meredith 1950–1954

Walter Bennett 1950–1966

Frederick Mills Welsford 1955–1964

Cecil George Gosling 1958–1971

Robert Bagshaw Wynne 1955–1964 (Dep Chair 1955–1963, MD 1960–1964, Chair 1963–1964)

P.A. Nash (Company Secretary) 1959–1963

William Bernard Ross Collins 1961–1964

Appointments after 1963

T.P. Jennison, Chairman 1964–1966

G.H. Tarrant 1964–?

Charles W. Powell, MD 1964–1969

J.L. Bush, Merchandise Director 1965–1969

Ivor Boyes, Merchandise Director 1965–1972

Jack Price, Financial Director 1965–1986

Charles Doerr 1965–?

Oswald Herbert, Production Director 1966–?

C. Gosling, Managing Director 1969–1972

Appointments after 1970

Ivor Boyes, Managing Director 1972–1975

Tony Gray, Merchandise Director 1972–1975 & 1981–1993

Tony Gray, Managing Director 1975–1981

Graham Newton, Merchandise Director 1975–1981

Gwyn Stevenson, Managing Director 1981–1996

John Simpson, Sales Director 1981–1989

Mike Moulds, Financial Director 1986–1996

Gary Spendlove, Sales Director 1993–1997

Bob Ash, Merchandise Director 1993–1997

APPENDIX 2

Assets and Profits

Ward Brettle & Ward

Year (y/e Dec)	Owed to Jn Ward	Net Assets £	Net Profit £	Rate %
1822	---------	93,634	(14,572)	(15.6)
1823	31,134	69,197	7,068	10.2
1824	25,978	84,352	15,154	17.9
1825	25,996	92,860	8,507	9.2
1826	25,669	104,836	11,974	11.4
1827	26,000	126,876	21,939	17.3
1829	26,000	161,044	17,083	10.6
1830	26,000	191,232	30,187	15.7
1831	26,000	215,947	24,713	11.4
1832	0	233,831	17,883	7.6

George Brettle & Co.

Year (y/e Dec)	Debts Due by company	Net Assets £	Sales £	Net Profit £	Rate %
1915	140,973	167,448	654,289	34,446	20.5
1916	58,528	201,746	610,577	34,298	17.0
1917	60,166	213,186	626,215	54,180	25.4
1918	68,598	267,390	898,108	95,966	35.8
1919	73,449	329,098	1,253,551	149,672	45.4
1920	197,619	351,111	1,563,093	141,119	40.1
1921	253,642	232,504	1,797,361	(103,836)	(44.6)
1922	163,248	232,505	1,108,094	(15,472)	(6.6)
1923	74,591	258,569	1,158,744	48,844	18.6
1924	71,739	274,541	1,096,191	29,408	10.7
1925	87,491	300,131	1,143,002	48,315	16.1
1926	97,552	309,965	1,233,929	41,267	13.3
1927	90,723	323,417	1,187,332	41,426	12.8
1928	99,276	347,770	1,204,775	53,699	15.4
1929	121,536	377,873	1,415,085	53,158	14.0
1930	117,257	395,441	1,484,340	49,278	12.4
1931	99,981	387,552	1,132,052	36,728	9.4
1932	80,421	382,604	1,172,199	28,381	7.4
1933	71,066	372,079	1,048,542	22,362	6.0
1934	76,341	372,681	1,066,497	22,990	6.1
1935	65,792	366,734	1,068,724	20,303	5-5
1936	70,078	363,795	1,043,703	18,289	5.0
1937	75,598	365,048	1,050,965	20,846	5.7
1938	67,721	364,964	1,053,790	22,189	6.0
1939	69,496	368,353	1,038,790	22,854	6.2
1940	79,904	385,080	1,220,697	36,981	9.6

APPENDIX 3

Sales by Department, George Brettle & Co.

In the early years, a high fraction of sales were wholesale, not actually produced by Brettles.

Year (y/e Dec)	Belper Cotton £	Other Cotton £	Belper Pants £	Other Pants £	Belper Produce £	Other Sales £	Total Sales £
1908	2,939	10,457	9,983	54,172	12,922	253,246	266,168
1909	3,529	10,701	9,934	55,314	13,463	270,035	283,498
1910	4,708	11,059	10,075	55,846	14,783	285,684	300,467
1911	7,270	10,203	8,237	26,263	15,507	306,222	321,729
1912	6,613	10,910	6,971	55,491	13,584	322,467	336,051

After 1912 it is not possible to distinguish between produce and non-produce, but closest comparative figures are given, plus a couple of new lines manufactured at Belper.

Year (y/e Dec)	All Cotton £	Under-Wear £	Ribbed U'wear £	Half Hose £	Total Sales £
1914	19,332	69,214	0	0	376,990
1915	21,320	162,169	0	0	654,289
1916	22,101	201,001	0	0	610,577
1917	30,161	135,237	25,979	0	626,215
1918	45,831	190,542	42,119	0	898,108
1919	55,218	241,948	59,032	0	1,253,551
1920	59,410	239,901	69,893	87,599	1,563,093
1921	76,541	249,638	81,906	130,878	1,797,361
1922	39,935	177,706	41,657	74,987	1,108,094
1923	43,790	210,413	50,416	83,013	1,158,744
1924	50,957	190,353	48,846	104,585	1,096,191
1925	59,942	188,429	47,700	124,478	1,143,002
1926	83,414	185,198	43,771	131,897	1,233,929
1927	99,285	171,216	36,300	124,427	1,187,332
1928	118,379	184,834	35,820	110,602	1,204,775
1929	139,094	189,491	43,530	113,874	1,415,085
1930	156,655	187,868	48,449	107,058	1,484,340
1931	131,767	185,313	39,140	86,944	1,132,052
1932	122,742	187,807	35,141	63,316	1,172,199
1933	108,818	155,497	30,914	54,519	1,048,542
1934	109,196	150,637	40,886	56,892	1,066,497
1935	102,627	147,374	43,186	57,917	1,068,724
1936	104,788	142,129	36,986	57,973	1,043,703
1937	112,625	140,149	39,071	59,625	1,050,965
1938	113,355	139,716	39,985	61,572	1,053,790
1939	119,318	144,199	36,641	61,663	1,038,790
1940	127,379	208,109-	44,545	63,355	1,220,697

APPENDIX 4

Key Indicators for George Brettle & Co. Ltd

Year (y/e Dec)	Net Assets £	Production £	Sales £	Net Profit £	Rate %
1941	396,551	?	1,201,162	30,473	7.6
1942	408,711	?	753,164	31,162	7.6
1943	410,266	254,286	620,293	30,058	7.3
1944	411,020	231,110	646,738	29,793	7.2
1945	411,514	235,570	674,123	29,535	7.1
1946	411,451	227,464	649,657	28,977	7.0
1947	430,609	270,528	780,362	31,214	7.2
1948	438,807	315,673	932,475	42,308	9.6
1949	493,434	428,674	1,283,502	54,409	11.0
1950	554,467	514,241	1,530,000	59,245	10.6
1951	620,848	630,016	1,883,739	88,099	14.1
1952	652,061	758,893	2,104,757	78,440	12.0
1953	620,631	547,517	1,637,859	48,794	7.8
1954	740,490	727,343	2,054,206	109,673	14.8
1955	800,733	820,785	2,198,604	126,298	15.7
1956	839,104	770,575	2,117,619	113,223	13.4
1957	823,241	701,346	2,024,358	70,066	8.5
1958	824,781	764,937	1,948,774	60,877	7.3
1959	807,373	594,475	1,850,402	40,817	5.0
1960	800,949	?	1,826,597	53,329	6.6
1961	824,653	?	1,959,513	75,985	9.2
1962	846,695	?	1,992,007	61,823	7.3
1963	832,451	?	2,053,225	52,981	6.3
1964	787,271	?	?	14,305	1.8

INDEX

Published in the UK by:
Slenderella Limited
Queen Street
Belper DE56 1NR

Tel: 01773 822340
E-mail: info@slenderella.co.uk

1st edition

ISBN: 978 184306 533 3 Paperback

ISBN: 978 184306 534 0 Hardback